A Mind to Stay Here

A Mind to Stay Here

Profiles from the South

by John Egerton

WITH PHOTOGRAPHS BY *Al Clayton*

The Macmillan Company
Collier-Macmillan Ltd., London

ACKNOWLEDGMENTS

Portions of this book appeared previously, in somewhat different form, in *The New South:*

The chapter on Will Campbell was in vol. 22, no. 4, Fall 1967.

The chapter on James McBride Dabbs was in vol. 24, no. 1,
Winter 1969.

The Macmillan Company
866 Third Avenue, New York, N.Y. 10022
Collier-Macmillan Canada Ltd., Toronto, Ontario

Library of Congress
Catalog Card Number: 70-115298

First Printing

Printed in the United States of America

For my mother, a gentle lady who stays here

Contents

Preface

Who remembers the South? It has changed, and it remains the same.

The civil-rights movement was a Southern phenomenon for more than a decade. Then came the Civil Rights Act of 1964, the anti-poverty program, the Voting Rights Act of 1965, the escalation of the war in Vietnam, "civil disorders" in Watts, Newark, Detroit and other cities, Black Power, the New Left, the assassination of Dr. Martin Luther King, campus unrest. The Movement has moved on, and there is a stillness at Selma, a tenuous truce in Mississippi, an uneasy quiet on the Southern front. Except for the persistent issue of school desegregation and the Nixon administration's "Southern strategy," the nation is preoccupied elsewhere; it looks away from Dixie.

But the South is still here. It is in ferment, yet it is still what it always was: a land full of human beings, diverse and contradictory and unpredictable. The South has been analyzed, dissected, and interpreted by critics and scholars and apologists for more than three centuries. It has all been recorded—the South of slavery, of civil war, of reconstruction, of segregation and white supremacy, the South of the civil-rights era. In all that, the region's evils have stood out like raw sores, and the evils were real—*are* real—and no amount of rationalizing or romanticizing can explain them away. But the South is more than that. It is not a monolith, and it never was; and while its virtues and its saving graces have often been obscured by the enormity of its sins, they have been here all along.

This is a book about a few Southerners who differ from the common stereotype. They also differ from one another, but they do have some things in common: they were born and raised in the South, and still live here; they are characterized more by their individuality than by their identity with any group or organization; the conventional labels—radical, liberal, moderate, conservative—fit them poorly, if at all; they are peaceful people in a violent world; they believe in human equality, and they live their lives in keeping with that belief.

None of them are nationally famous personalities whose names have become household words in all parts of the country, although some of them are well known in the circles in which they move. They live in nine of the eleven states of the Old Confederacy; they are young and old, black and white, male and female; and they fall somewhere between comfortable affluence and the borderlines of poverty. They are living Southerners who remain in the South, and for whom being Southern is not merely incidental—it is a big part of who and what they are.

Insofar as they are alike, these people represent a side of the South that has been written about too little—in a word, the non-racist South. But they and their region are too complex to be described in generalized phrases, and "non-racist" is such a phrase.

The profiles have been written over the past three years, and are based on personal acquaintance with the people, on conversations with them, on books and articles by and about them, and on remembrances of others who know them well. They are not full-blown portraits or definitive biographies

—they are simply sketches, enhanced by the clarity and sensitivity of Al Clayton's photographs.

It will be obvious to the reader that I have written about people whom I admire and respect and appreciate, and there is danger in this. There is, first of all, the danger of overdrawing the sketches in heroic dimensions, out of proportion to reality. And, because the profiles are based primarily upon contact with the people being written about, there is the danger that they will appear as contributors to a favorable and sympathetic retelling of their lives, as parties to whatever distortion there may be. There is also the danger that a book about a few people, no matter how they have been chosen, will leave the impression that they are somehow unique, an elite group having special virtues and qualities not found in many others. And finally, there is the danger that such a book distorts the South by putting a face on it that is unrepresentative.

To the first, I can only say that I have tried to tell, honestly and accurately, about these people as I see them. They are interesting characters, but they are not saints— they are all too human, like the rest of us—and it is about their humanity that I have tried to write.

The second point can be disposed of quickly: what I have written is my interpretation, not theirs, and I assume full responsibility for it.

As for the third danger, my selection of these particular people to write about was as accidental as it was methodical. I don't claim for them—and they don't claim for themselves—any elitism or uniqueness or superior virtue. I am acutely conscious of the fact that hundreds, perhaps thousands, of others could have been written about, people who, in large ways and small, have tried to be honest and inclusive in their human relationships. I might have chosen some whose involvement in civil rights has been more extensive, or whose convictions have been more costly to them, or whose achievements appear more impressive. But any selection would be subject to the same limitations, and perhaps that is really the only point that can be made from all this: that there is in the South a rich variety of people who are not susceptible to facile stereotyping.

The final danger—that of distorting the South, of romanticizing it—is not a new one. In books and movies and plays and songs and speeches, the region's worst evils often have been glossed over by people who could not or would not face the ugly truth. I have no interest in gilding the lily-white traditions of the past. Since the coming of the first white men, the degrading and inhuman treatment of Negroes (and Indians, and often poor whites, too) has dominated life in the South, and no cosmetic reconstruction of history, however embellished, can put a pretty face on that. Yet this flawed land has managed somehow to retain some admirable human qualities that are uniquely characteristic. In spite of slavery and segregation and white supremacy, in spite of the gaping contrast between privilege and poverty, the South has produced in its history many men and women who have stood against those evils. I have written with a view of such people and such qualities, not to be an apologist for the worst of my native land but simply to say that the worst is not all there is to it.

All of the contradictions of the human condition have been graven indelibly on the many faces of the South. Hate and fear and evil have been conspicuous on those faces, but they are not the whole story. Perhaps there is a natural law of compensation which produces a human antidote for inhumanity. Whatever the case, there are in the South—as there have been through the decades—men and women who celebrate both the diversity and the equality of the human race. Many of them have said the South is different from the rest of the country, but often more in positive than in negative ways. They have said that human understanding across race and class lines may be more possible here than in other sections of the country. They have said that in spite of its

sins—or maybe, in some inexplicable way, because of them
—the South could be the birthplace of genuine human
equality in this country. Whether any of those things
actually are true cannot be proved, of course. They can only
be felt in some vague and instinctive way, or taken on faith.
But the people who keep calling the South to a realization
of its potential are not just whistling Dixie; they have some
convincing arguments on their side.

The people I have written about can be identified in a
general way with these beliefs. They are people who live in
the South, who love it, and who believe in racial reconciliation. Some of them believe the South has assets which could
be turned to the cause of human equality. They hold no
grand visions of a millennium here, but they would be poor
candidates for an Exodus, because they don't believe there
is a Promised Land somewhere over the mountains or across
the river, somewhere outside the South. Maybe all they are
saying is that the South is home. This is a book about those
people and the land they call home.

Nashville, 1970   JOHN EGERTON

I have a mind to stay here,
And a mind to leave this town.

—*The Freight Train Blues*

Will Campbell

That Mississippi magic is Mississippi madness now,
Yea, that Mississippi magic is Mississippi madness now.
Whites don't like black people,
Black don't like white nohow.

Will Davis Campbell, poet, prophet and preacher-at-large, sat under the tin roof of his farmhouse porch and cradled a Gibson guitar in his lap. In a deep, melancholy voice he was singing a "country-folk" ballad of his own creation, and it embraced, as no description could, the theology and the personality of the man himself.

It was pure, undistilled Will, the essence. A tan leather strap, bearing the words "Will D. Campbell" in raised letters, held the guitar suspended from his stooped shoulders. His faded Lee overall pants had holes in the knees and his blue shirt was open at the collar. An empty fruit jar stood sentry beside his tapping cowboy boot, and Dottie, his Dalmatian, kept trying to climb up beside him on the old church pew where he sat.

As I watched and listened, the question kept echoing in my mind: "Who is this guy? Who the hell *is* Will Campbell?"

It wasn't the first time I had wondered. Sometimes I think I know the answer, and sometimes I'm sure I don't.

There are, of course, some obvious answers. He is a devoted husband and father of three children. He is a Mississippi-born Baptist preacher. He is a farmer and a writer. He is at least an acquaintance and at best a valued friend and adviser of a goodly number of the men and women, black and white, who constituted what was known as "The Move-ment," the civil-rights movement, before it came unglued.

But none of that says who Will Campbell is. The song he was singing tells about a man who left Mississippi on the Illinois Central railroad, met a woman in Chicago, and vowed he was never going back. In a Tex Ritter-style talking verse, Will tells what happens then:

She say, "Where you from, sport, Mis'sippi?"
Say, "Yea, that's right. Mis'sippi."
She say, "Why ain't you goin' back? You like the Nigras or the Kluxers?"
I say, "I like the Nigras *and* the Kluxers."
She say, "What are you, some kind of a liberal?"
Say, "No, doll, I ain't no liberal. I just like everybody. And the Nigras and the Kluxers is somebody."

He sings the refrain, and then picks up the story again:

She say, "Hold on, sport, what about when you dead? You goin' back then?"
"Yea, goin' back then. Goin' back home! Say, "They gonna love me when I'm dead."
She say, "No, man. They ain't never gonna love you. You better stay up here and lie beside me."
"O yea. They gonna love me when I'm dead. They gonna come in from miles around—that old Hartmann Funeral Home in McComb City, stand 'round my coffin all night. An' they'll say, 'Ole Will was a good ole boy. He just had some crazy ideas.' "

The refrain is a little different this time:

Then that Mississippi madness, be Mississippi magic again.
Yea, that Mississippi madness, be Mississippi magic again.
'Fore we was born we was all kin.
When we dead we'll be kinfolks again.*

There's a final line or two, with Uncle Bob Tarver shaking his head and saying, "Don't he look natural," and Aunt Susie saying, "Law, Jesus, just like he oughta talk," and then Will plays something else, or quits and sticks a wad of chewing tobacco in his mouth. He had said as much as he is going to say about himself, and no further questions, however tactful, will get a response.

I've wanted to know who Will Campbell is ever since I first met him in 1965. He had an office in an old house in Nashville, across the street from where I had just gone to work, and though he has since moved to another location, I still see a good bit of him. Standing slump-shouldered or walking with an unhurried shuffle, he looks older than his forty-six years, but his uniform—disguise is perhaps a better word—effectively presents him as a country cousin duded up for a trip to town. The boots—always the boots—and a cane, selected from the dozens that fill a nail keg sitting in the corner of his living room, are stock accessories. Then there are the Western-cut suits, the gaudy shirts, the outlandish ties. Something about the shape of his face and the way his hair has receded in a palm-length retreat to the crown of his head reminds me of William Jennings Bryan or Adlai Stevenson—in some ways, his resemblance to both men is not only physical but philosophical.

Will is the director of an outfit called the Committee of Southern Churchmen, a nondenominational alliance of clergymen and laymen whose creed is taken from the fifth chapter of Second Corinthians:

*Copyright 1969 by United Artists Music, 7299 7th Ave., New York, N.Y. Used by permission.

For the love of Christ leaves us no choice when once we have reached the conclusion that one man died for all and therefore all mankind has died. His purpose in dying for all was that men, while still in life, should cease to live for themselves, and should live for him who for their sake died and was raised to life. With us therefore worldly standards have ceased to count in our estimate of any man. . . . We come therefore as Christ's ambassadors. It is as if God were appealing to you through us: In Christ's name, we implore you, be reconciled to God!

The key word is "reconciled." *Katallagete,* a Greek word meaning, "Be reconciled"—or as Will translates it, "Be what you are"—is the name of a magazine which he and his amorphous committee publish sporadically, and the committee itself is a reincarnation of the Fellowship of Southern Churchmen, which was born during the Depression years of the 1930s.

Though he was not a part of that early movement, Will Campbell is the voice—some would say the heart and soul—of the Committee of Southern Churchmen. To get a grasp of what that means, you have to go back a bit.

The place to start is on the Liberty, Mississippi, farm of Lee Webb Campbell and his wife, Hancie. Will and his three brothers and sisters were born there—Will in 1924—and they hoed cotton, went to school and joined the church at the time and in the manner expected of them. Will was ordained in the East Fork Baptist Church while he was still in high school. Then he went to Louisiana College for a year, served three years in the Army (he was a medic in the South Pacific), married a Louisiana girl named Brenda Fisher, spent three years getting an A.B. degree in English from Wake Forest College, did a year of graduate work at Tulane, went to Yale for three years and then, armed with a B.D. degree and plenty of eager enthusiasm, became the preacher of a 300-member Baptist church in the lumber mill community of Taylor, Louisiana, near the Mississippi border.

That lasted two and a half years. Then came two years as director of religious life at the University of Mississippi. In 1956 he opened a Southern office for the Racial and Cultural Relations Department of the National Council of Churches, and seven years later became director of the Committee of Southern Churchmen when it was reorganized.

That, in barest outline, is where he has been. What he has done can't be pinned down so precisely, but a lot of conversations with a lot of people, including him, help to fill in the picture.

Once I went to Mississippi with him in his tomato-red Ford pickup. He keeps his cane in a gun rack mounted over the rear window and spits tobacco juice in Coke bottles that lay scattered, with old copies of *Katallagete*, in the floor of the cab. For two days we rode and talked and argued. Here, in part, is what I learned:

Taylor, Louisiana, was a company town, and Will was a naïve country preacher who believed in the fatherhood of God and the brotherhood of man. The people were proud to have "one of the three Yale preachers in the whole state of Louisiana," and they let him get away with it when he talked about Negroes as part of the brotherhood. "It was before 1954, and that kind of talk was still a novelty." But Will was interested in applying the church's preachments, in matching deeds with words, and by the fall of 1954 he felt the need to move on.

"I wasn't any crusading radical by any means, but I wanted to work for the implementation of the Supreme Court's school desegregation decision—it was right, necessary and just—and I knew it would take at least ten years even if everyone was willing." (That was sixteen years ago; until this year, more than 90 per cent of Mississippi's Negro school children were still segregated.) For all his non-militancy, Will was a good eight years ahead of the Movement when he went to Ole Miss, and his Mississippi credentials didn't help at all. In the eyes of the "Never"-sayers, he was the only thing worse than an outside agitator: an inside traitor. He visited his old friend Gene Cox at Providence Farm, a Negro-white cooperative in Holmes County, and was duly reported to an irate legislature; he invited a liberal clergyman from the North to take part in Religious Emphasis Week, only to have the university chancellor cancel the appearance; and to top it all off, he played ping pong in the campus YMCA building with a Negro minister friend of his.

When he was reprimanded for that last indiscretion, Will asked his superior, the university vice chancellor, "How much longer do we go on 'adjusting' in the name of education, of the greater good? We've taken the loyalty oath, listed the organizations we've belonged to in the past, let the American Legion screen our visiting speakers. How much longer? It's hard to adjust to barbed wire."

A few nights later, at a reception at the Y (which Will also headed), somebody dumped human feces in the punch bowl. After he discovered it, Will marched the vice chancellor over to the bowl and asked him, "Are you going to adjust to fecal punch?" "He had once been J. Edgar Hoover's chief assistant and could smell out a subversive anywhere, but he couldn't find out who crapped in the YMCA punch." The chancellor used to tell him, "Will, we'll stand and fight at the proper time, but this is just not the ditch to die in. When the time comes for you to leave, we'll all march across that bridge together." After the feces, Will's time had come, but it still was not the chancellor's ditch, and Will walked across the bridge alone.

That was in 1956. The shock of *Brown vs. Board of Education* was beginning to sink in, and the first brush fires of social change were popping out in places like Sturgis, Kentucky, and Clinton, Tennessee. The National Council of Churches, seeking a role for itself in the developing drama, decided to set up a Southern office of its race relations division, and Will was asked to head it. He moved his family to

Nashville, and for the next seven years he was the NCC's man in the South. This is how he describes that experience:

> The Council hired me and turned me loose. They didn't know what to tell me to do, so we got along fine. Later on, when they did start telling me what to do, we had troubles. But in the beginning I was a kind of troubleshooter, a mediator. I just went where the trouble was—Little Rock, New Orleans, Montgomery, Birmingham—and I stayed out of the center of things, out of the spotlight. No speeches, no press releases. In Little Rock I got my name in the papers because three of us walked to school with the Negro children. After that, I avoided publicity and spent my time operating between and among organizations and factions, instead of in them.

As time passed, Will's reputation as a mediator, strategist and adviser grew among such disparate groups as SNCC, SCLC, NAACP, the church, the press and the power structures of a score of Southern communities. He was a confidant of Negroes on the firing line, a trusted source for the working press, a man who could sit on a cabin porch and pray with troubled parents as easily as he could sit in the Establishment's paneled board room and tell the powers how to end the trouble. He was his own man, belonging to no one, having no vested interests to protect. And he was effective.

> My role shifted drastically when the churches began to join the marches. All of a sudden here were white militants of another sort. The NCC became another "God is on our side" faction, just like the white segregationists. I have a distrust of the white liberal who says, "behave and act like us." I didn't want to be identified with a white liberal-dominated movement. They were working for the church, when they should have been working for the faith. The church as an institution could collapse tomorrow and it wouldn't matter. I was never a part of the civil-rights movement, I didn't work in race relations, I wasn't a social engineer—I was, and I am, a preacher.

Everybody, I suppose, is trying to decide who God is. Well, God is not the church, or politics, or civil rights, or liberalism, though all of these have been held up as the savior, the solution, the panacea. But God is not me or you, or anything any of us can create. God is no cause, no movement. And all this leaves you is to proclaim what has been done for you. But the idea of something having been accomplished by the incarnation is anathema to these people. They're still building temples.

He was a thorn in the flesh. His boss finally told him, "We can't pay a man a salary just to preach," and Will's response was, "Then you can't pay me a salary to do anything." He left the NCC, and the remnant of the Fellowship of Southern Churchmen, with modest financial support from three foundations, revitalized their little organization and got Will to run it. He bought himself a 20-acre farm near Mt. Juliet, 25 miles from downtown Nashville, and for the past seven years he has been doing for the resurrected Committee of Southern Churchmen what he started out doing for the National Council of Churches.

I got most of this from him while we rode through the Mississippi countryside. We talked theology, too, both then and on other occasions, and I have read in *Katallagete* and in his book, *Race and the Renewal of the Church,* what amounts to his "position." The theology of Will Campbell is unstructured, simple, fundamental, and profound. It is also radical, complex, and compelling. It is two parts Paul and one part Barth, an unlikely combination of Yale Divinity School and East Fork Baptist Church. You can find in it a little situation ethics, some agnosticism, a dash of literalism and a mixture of Reinhold Niebuhr, A. J. Muste and Billy Graham. In short, it fits none of the molds.

Will states it this way: "I believe in God, and I believe Christ was God—though it's not necessary for me to accept the divinity of Christ in order to believe in God. I don't know who or what God is—I have no theories about any of that. When I use the word 'God,' that's as far as I can go. It's a way of saying I don't know the answers. Do I pray? Every thought is a prayer. So is saying, 'I believe in God.' "

About such things as the virgin birth, the resurrection, life after death and so forth, he takes no dogmatic position. "It all seems beside the point to me," he says. "There is a God, and he takes care of such things. I don't bother with them. It's as far as I can go to believe there is a perfect God, beyond my understanding, and he has made us free and fallible—for what reasons I couldn't say."

He is no proselytizer, yet in his way he is very much an evangelist. Will has a message, but it isn't delivered from the stump, and it doesn't rain down the fear of God upon the unwashed. For a man who believes in the inherently evil nature of man, he is curiously uncritical of men. His message is not so much, "Repent and be saved," as it is, "You are forgiven; God does not hold your misdeeds against you" —though he doesn't think the two can be separated.

In the first issue of *Katallagete* in 1965, Will wrote of a kind of evangelism that would serve as an alternative to the status-quo posture of most churches, on the one hand, and the uncritical commitment to revolution, on the other. In later issues he wrote of "the failure of law in the racial crisis," and of the failure of the church as an institution. Of Thomas Coleman, the slayer of Episcopalian seminarian Jonathan Daniels, he wrote:

> When Thomas killed Jonathan he committed a crime against the state of Alabama. Alabama, for reasons of its own, chose not to punish him for that crime against itself. . . . When Thomas killed Jonathan he committed a crime against God. The strange, the near maddening thing about this case is that both these offended parties have rendered the same verdict—not for the same reasons, not in the same way, but the verdict is the same—acquittal.

In his book on race and the church, published by West-minster Press in 1962, the dominant theme is "Thus saith the Lord! Not, Thus saith the Law!" Will questions whether "we" are still the church, suggesting that God has perhaps turned to other vehicles because we have denied him. We self-righteously condemn the segregationist, he says, yet our own lives are a denial of reconciliation because we classify and categorize people according to our own prejudices. All of us, segregationists and integrationists alike, claim both God and the law are on our side.

The church, he continues, must concern itself not with laws or humanism but with the gospel. "The Christian must first of all be concerned with souls." He must minister not only to the dispossessed, but to the dispossessors. Will writes of the "broken heart-repentance-forgiveness-reconciliation-renewal sequence that expresses the order of salvation." He rejects the theological liberalism which puts man at the center of life, capable of perfection: "Our problem is that we have spoken too much of man's worth and dignity and not often enough of his insignificance in God's scheme of things." Both the Bible and secular history show, he says,

> that life is suffering and sorrow and the beginning of death; that we all come forth like a flower and are cut down; that we are all of a few days and full of trouble; that all flesh is grass and we are all here dying together. What man can face this truth and continue to see the relevance of human classifications of people into colors and races?

Will Campbell is a pessimist, a fatalist, an apocalyptic prophet of doom. He is, at the same time, more radical than the most extreme liberal. He speaks to the intelligentsia, the ones who have chucked the church as unrealistic, hypocritical, materialistic, status crazy, and dishonest, and tells them that faith is something more, much more, than just the church. He speaks to the fundamentalist, telling him that faith is not simply fatalism and literalism and fear. And he speaks to the mass of casual Christians in between, telling them that their church has become a club, an exclusive organization, and it will eventually collapse of its own weight. His theology can't be systematized, it isn't consistent, but then, in a world of fallible men, nothing is really systematic or consistent.

Milton Mayer, writing in *The Progressive* about the late A. J. Muste, described him in words that fit Will Campbell like a glove:

> Let him [Muste] be a lesson to those who are young in heart and full of beans and will soon be old in heart and full of resentment. For all that they do—or just as well don't do— they will leave the world no better than they found it. They will have their hands full leaving things no worse. This was A. J.'s puny triumph . . . he held his own. . . . A. J. believed that a man had no call to be effective; what he was called to be was right. He was never disenchanted with men, because he was never enchanted by them. He was never demoralized, because he did not live by morality. He never despaired of the world, because he did not live by the world.
>
> What he lived by was the old-time religion of Christ crucified and risen. . . .

That was Muste according to Mayer, and it is also Will Campbell. His theology is that he has none—no rules, no creeds, no thou-shalt-nots. Just this: You are forgiven. This man who disclaims the perfectibility of all men has an abiding faith that anyone who hears and believes that he is truly forgiven will not use that pardon as license to keep on practicing inhumanity on his fellow man—and that is only one of the paradoxes that dominate his personality. Will sees human failure in himself and in others without becoming cynical; he is a thinker with the breadth of vision to see the big picture but he is not an intellectual; and at the most unlikely times his pungent humor pierces through his despair.

Like the time in 1964 when he had a serious operation. After the danger had passed and he was making a satisfactory recovery, his doctor informed him that his heart had stopped while he was on the table. "How long was I dead?" Will asked, and the doctor told him it had taken about three minutes to get his heart started again.

"If you could certify that it was three *days,* Doc, that would solve the problem of leadership in my outfit," Will said.

His "outfit," his following, his people, include seminarians at Harvard, Yale, Union, Vanderbilt, and elsewhere who are confronted on occasion by Will Campbell, preacher-at-large, wandering minstrel, an irreverent and impious missionary in a cowboy suit. He can be humorous, witty, sarcastic, laughing at his audience, or with them, or at himself, but even through the laughter his message gets nailed to the seminary wall, and it stays there to disturb and discomfort long after he has spit tobacco juice in the dusty cloisters and gone.

Will was traveling that circuit when the civil-rights movement was just beginning. What is happening in civil rights has been called a revolution, he told them, but it is not. We have had a little—but only a very little—social reform; the revolution is yet to come. The social reformers—the Kings, the Wilkinses, the Farmers—have not been able to bring us whites to the realization that our denial of rights to the dispossessed can only lead to the destruction of all rights. The true revolutionaries are waiting in the wings. Their success has already been assured by white stupidity. The revolutionaries are suspicious, even contemptuous, of white liberals, who, when revolution comes, will be the first to go. We don't really know how out of touch, how irrelevant, we are.

The only course for a Christian in all this, he said, is to live and act as reconciled, forgiven children of God, and to take that gospel of forgiveness to the alienated. He must reject the status quo, which is defended by those who have, in a belated and probably futile effort to make unnecessary the revolution of hate and despair by those who have not. And if it is already too late, if the oppression cannot be removed and redressed, well, there is no other choice. The message has been around for 2,000 years. We can only repeat it, and hope.

Sobering stuff. And prophetic. Will was saying it a decade

ago, when people like Whitney Young and Roy Wilkins were commonly considered dangerous radicals, and nobody knew Stokely Carmichael's name.

Elbert Jean is a Methodist minister from the rural South who worked for a time with Will in the early 1960s and remains a close friend of his. Elbert likes to talk about Will's "deliverance from organization," his "sentiment and sensitivity," and he speaks with admiration about "this little boy at heart, this little ole boy from down in Amite County who wants to play cowboy, who's not a scholar in any sense but is about the most undisciplined fellow you're likely to run across."

Elbert Jean says Will's itinerant ministry in the South's racial trouble spots took him "to the ones who were under attack. He would go and just sit with them, not knowing what to say, just being afraid with them, mainly. Will has a demeanor that allows him to gain confidence on both sides. He's not as much of a direct fighter, he doesn't go out and try to brawl with folks, but he is extremely effective—almost Machiavellian, I believe—in knowing how to move city governments and state politicians and power structures in a favorable direction." And, says Elbert,

> He has this sensitivity that kinda says it's enough to be a person. This is his faith, his theology, if you please. He believes God loves us as much when we're bad as when we're good. He doesn't worry very much about folks' morals. He is the one person I've met in race relations who has this orientation. Everybody else has some kind of ax to grind or some kind of cause to promote. Will just says if you're a human being, if you're a person, well, you're in. The reason Will hasn't joined the civil-rights movement—or they haven't joined him—is that he's too radical for them.

Some people see Will as nothing more than a buffoon, but the late Thomas Merton, the Trappist monk and writer, had a deeper insight. "I think he is somebody that people need to know about," Merton once said. "He is deeply and thoroughly Christian with a kind of Christianity that does not take refuge in irrelevancy . . . a true Southerner who wants the word of God to be heard without muffling and without distortion in the South so that hatred and bloodshed may be replaced by reconciliation and brotherhood. I admire his humor, his humanity, and his faith."

James Y. Holloway, a professor of ethics at Berea College and editor of *Katallagete*, calls Will "the most genuinely respected person I have ever known in the areas of his own ministry: the broken racial and personal relations in the South and in the nation." Holloway says Will takes the Christian faith at face value. "He sees men—not the abstracted, generalized, non-men–non-entities of the theologians and philosophers and social 'scientists,' but Kluxers and Movement men and the childish New Left and the sophisticated Old Right and the selfish and priests and liberal pastors and segregationist preachers—as sinners who have been, are, right this moment, reconciled to God in Christ."

And Johnny Popham, managing editor of the *Chattanooga Times,* has another view. "Flannery O'Connor's short stories tell about people trapped in tragedy," he says. "Will Campbell rescues her victims."

I have heard Will described in a lot of ways, but for sheer poetry none can match this from James McBride Dabbs, when he was president of the Committee of Southern Churchmen:

> There's no way to capture Will in words; you just have to take him round and show him off, cowboy boots and cane and vest. Or, if you're going to use words, you just have to be outrageous with them. Say Will is quicksilver. No matter how many pieces he breaks into, every one is Will happily running around. Or say he's an actor and conclude there's no real Will; every face he puts on is a fake. Or say he's that special kind of actor we call clown: the painted smile hiding the broken heart.

Will once did me the honor of including me in one of his devastating comments. He had just said that in the Christian view all men are bastards, but God loves them just the same. Somewhat doubtful, I replied, "That may be true, Will, but somehow I seem to be a happy bastard." He almost ran his Mercedes off the Cumberland Plateau. Waving both hands, he said, "Ah, that's the worst kind! The very worst kind!" The more I think about it, the more I think he was unconsciously describing himself. That's why he was so sure.

"Like a bat out of hell." In a sense this is Will. Forever exploding upward from the flames, lit from the fires beneath but beginning to take the sunlight overhead. And then, almost before we know it, he is the skylark, lost in the blue, and singing. . . .

The bat exploding out of hell and the skylark poised at the zenith, Will is both, and both are the same, and both are Everyman. That's the kind of game he's playing. He wants to be everybody! (This may be a reaction from Mississippi, where everybody wants to be nobody.) . . .

The Greeks put Socrates to death because he asked too many questions. Will doesn't ask many questions, but he makes us ask them, and that's worse. Whatever happens to him, he's got it coming. As he himself would say, he's a questionable character.

Where do you go to find out who Will Campbell is? You can try places like the Southern Regional Council, the Southern Christian Leadership Conference, the Southern Student Organizing Committee or the American Friends Service Committee. You can ask a New York foundation executive, or a North Carolina Klansman, or a Congressman in Washington, or a mill hand in Louisiana. There are housewives and newspapermen who know him, tenant farmers and attorneys, shopkeepers and university professors, musicians and doctors and ministers. I have talked to a lot of them. A few, like James McBride Dabbs, are eloquent; most are at a loss for words.

Much of what you see on his farm in the valley fits somewhere in the collage that is Will Campbell's portrait. The menagerie of pets with names like Ralph and Dottie and Leon and Fanny Hill and Cecil and Zack, the canes in the nail keg, the shelves of books that line the wall, the little log cabin across the creek where he goes to write, the guitar, the corn growing in the bottom and the corn bottled on the shelf, the parables of the spirit told in words of the earth— they're all part of the trappings that help to reveal, or help to disguise, the real Will.

There is just one other thing I have found that sheds light on him. It is a speech he made to a group of college students he shepherded through a human-relations seminar for the National Student Association a few summers ago. In it are parts of the poet, the prophet, the preacher:

> . . . we arrived with an assumed sophistication in the area of human relations. If any hint of that sophistication remains, the seminar has failed you, for in the field of human relations sophistication is indeed "a delusion, a mockery and a snare." For human relations, you see, is about humans, and humans are mighty strange creatures indeed, and the more you learn about them the more confused you become. There are no authorities, no experts in the field, for the variables of society are too numerous and the exigencies of history are too unpredictible for a science ever to evolve out of our endeavors. . . . Why did we come here? In six years of moving into the various racial crises of the South, I have asked myself that many times. I do not have an answer, but I believe it is because somewhere along the way I began to feel the tragedy of the South—indeed, the tragedy of human existence—and I keep trying because I have no choice under God but to behave as if the whole burden rests on my shoulders, knowing all the while that in six years I cannot see one thing I have personally accomplished. So must you behave—as if you will single-handedly solve all her woes—but you must know that there will be times when all your human efforts, all strategies, all techniques, all movements will fail; all human engineering will go lame, and only your understanding of the tragedy

will remain—only your broken heart, your ability to weep—
because you have the capacity to understand.

. . . Human relations . . . is not a new field. It has been
going on since tribal savages screamed over the hills through
the night to the cave of another tribe and sought to destroy
them—not because they were different . . . not because they
were dangerous to him . . . but just because they were there.

But one morning coming home from battle one of those
primitive savages stooped over and picked something up. . . .
It was a feather blowing along the beach. It wasn't worth a
thing—it was just pretty. He took it back to his cave and kept
it because it spoke to his deepest feelings. But soon he found
that its beauty spoke forth only if he shared it with his fellows and with his brothers. With this feather, civilization
began and human relations began.

. . . we still storm through the night, over vast oceans and
over narrow lunch counters . . . with H-bombs and lead pipes
and small baseball bats, with legislation and propaganda,
closed schoolhouses, burning churches. . . .

Human relations is still, as then, the display of a feather—
the effort to say there is some other way. . . .

Adlai Stevenson came across that speech and was so impressed by it that he had it copied and circulated it among
some of his friends.

Who knows Will Campbell, who understands him? One
of the things he is trying to do is to establish a ministry to
a group of Ku Klux Klansmen—not to reform them, not to
change them, not to make them "act like us," but simply to
tell them, "We are all bastards, but God loves us anyway."
Some time ago, his friendship with the Klansmen was related
to a middle-class intellectual and his wife by a friend who
was introducing them to Will.

"How do you manage to communicate with those people?"
the lady asked him.

"By emptying their bedpans," Will answered.

> No, doll, I ain't no liberal. I just like everybody.
> And the Nigras and the Kluxers is somebody.

James McBride Dabbs

The civil-rights movement was a traveling road show that held center stage before massed crowds of the hopeful and the hostile during a twelve-year run in the South. For sheer drama, it was unsurpassed; the emotional fervor whipped up by fire-eyed evangelists on the Sawdust Trail in an earlier day seems by comparison as quiet and placid as a Sunday night vespers. The Movement had all the elements of a great folk epic—heroes and villains, triumphs and tragedies, martyrs and prophets, a supreme cause (integration), and a cast of thousands.

Historians will probably quibble over the dates, but those who like specific beginnings and endings will likely choose May 17, 1954, as the start of the Movement and June 26, 1966, as its finish. On the first date, the U.S. Supreme Court declared school segregation laws unconstitutional; on the second, James Meredith's "march against fear" ended at the Mississippi capital in Jackson, and the rallying cry of "black power" was firmly established by Stokely Carmichael and other militant leaders. Since then, the stage has shifted to the cities of the North, the cast of characters has changed, and the old cause has been widely disavowed. But in the years spanned by those two dates, the issues in dispute were reasonably clear and simple, the proponents and opponents of equality for black Americans were visible and outspoken, and the South was the scene.

From the earliest days of the movement—indeed, long before it began—there were Southerners who saw more logic than accident in the fact that the South had spawned the Negro's drive for equality. This, they felt, was where it *had* to begin, but more: this small and scattered group of men and women believed that the South was where it could succeed, not only first but more fully.

I have never met many Northerners or Westerners who understood that. The notion that the South, where Negroes were systematically dehumanized and where white supremacy still has not surrendered its hold, could somehow be the place where equality and justice might first be attained in this country is a laughable absurdity to most non-Southerners—and perhaps to a majority of Southerners as well.

But there are those, in residence and in exile, who believe it. They are lawyers and teachers, social workers and community organizers, preachers and farmers and laborers— men and women, sophisticated and simple, black and white. Their convictions are expressed matter-of-factly, or hopefully, or bitterly, in intellectual terms of reason and logic or with uncluttered simplicity. Whether they hold it as a gut feeling, an article of faith, or an inescapable reality, these deep-rooted and uprooted Southerners share the belief that the key to racial reconciliation in America—if there is a key—will be found in the South. They have no movement, they are not of one mind, and some of them have little in common except that conviction, but they can be heard quietly expressing it or ruefully admitting it in places like New York and New Orleans, Berkeley and Birmingham, Cambridge and St. Louis and Newark and Little Rock—and Mayesville, South Carolina.

James McBride Dabbs lives not far from Mayesville. He is a farmer, writer, former professor and a country gentleman, and at seventy-four he is an elder statesman in that vague and amorphous category labeled "Southern liberal." He was nearing sixty when the civil-rights movement began, and in his own style he devoted himself to it. In magazine articles and speeches, in three books, in the presidency of the Southern Regional Council, and in the (Southern) Presbyterian Church's deliberations and pronouncements on social matters he has spoken with candor and conviction about the South.

In the tumult of 1970, the South is hardly in the picture, except where school desegregation is concerned. The compelling national issues now are Vietnam and the cities and the environment, the New Left and the Renascent Right, law and order, police brutality, campus unrest, black separatism, violence. Except when George Wallace kindles the segregationist longings of his white following, or the black nationalists speak of carving a New Africa out of the Deep South, we are reminded but little that the national focus until four years ago was on racial discrimination in the South. They are seldom heard now, but Southerners like James M. Dabbs are still saying that the South, for all its problems, is still the most favorable setting for racial reconciliation.

Dabbs lives at Rip Raps Plantation, which is on a rural mail route out of Mayesville. The easiest way to get there is to take U.S. 378 east from Sumter, and 12 miles out turn abruptly to the right onto a sandy lane that cuts a straight course through the pines. It is like dusk under there; clusters of dark green needles and Spanish moss blot out the sky. The speck of white at the end of the lane, three-quarters of a mile away, grows larger and grayer as you approach it, and when you reach the clearing the gaunt and disheveled plantation house stands like an apparition, an ante-bellum relic that has fallen on hard times.

Rip Raps is an anachronism, a period piece lifted whole out of the stereotype of the Old South—not the movie-set

mansion with graceful white columns and broad porches on
all sides, but rather the solid, square, substantial home of a
successful plantation farmer. Dabbs has lived there since
1937—his grandfather built the house in 1860—and he was
born just a mile or so down the road. He went back there,
to the land of his youth, not with any notion of re-creating
the plantation way of life but simply to farm and write and
raise a family. He was forty-one, and had just given up the
chairmanship of the English department at Coker College in
Hartsville. In 1933, his first wife had died, leaving him with
two daughters, aged thirteen and two, and two years later
he had remarried. The return to Rip Raps was in a sense a
withdrawal, and if the old house was a reminder of a long-
gone way of life, it was also a spacious and comfortable and
familiar haven.

Dabbs continued to teach part-time at Coker until 1942,
and then for the next ten years or so he gave most of his
energies to making a living from the farm. By the early '50s,
civil rights was the South's gathering storm, and when it
broke, Dabbs had long since chosen his stance.

But that is getting ahead of the story. Dabb tells it himself with admirable skill in *The Road Home,* a kind of
philosophical autobiography, and in two volumes about his
native land, *The Southern Heritage* and *Who Speaks for
the South?* He talked about his books and his life and the
issues of civil rights when I went to Rip Raps in the shim-
mering heat of a July day. We settled into the cool stillness
of his cluttered and comfortable study, and he spoke in a
softly accented voice above the muted drone of a floor fan
and the distant whistling of jays and mockingbirds somewhere in the pines.

He talked about his father, a Scotch-Irish Puritan, proud
and hard-working, and his mother, a quiet, warm-hearted
person, and how their contrasting personalities shaped his
own. They stood at times in tension between the future and
the past, between the farm and the plantation, between

frankness and politeness, and James felt the pull of both personalities even after his mother died when he was thirteen.

He went to the University of South Carolina, then to Clark University in Massachusetts for a master's degree in psychology, and he married a schoolmate of one of his sisters. During World War I he served as a first lieutenant in the field artillery, and then he came back to South Carolina, where he farmed for a year and taught for four, the last three of them at the state university. Before going to Coker College, he studied for a doctorate in English at Columbia University and later went back there for a second year, but never completed the degree.

His wife was in poor health for most of their married life, and in the years just before and after her death, Dabbs brooded and agonized about the irony and tragedy of life. Then he remarried, and two years later moved to Rip Raps, back to the home of his mother's people, "a house weather-beaten in my boyhood, unpainted since 1860, looming gray among the trees, with tall columns and long halls, bitter cold in winter but deliciously cool on summer days . . . there was a certain spaciousness there, partly physical, as of broad piazzas and halls, partly spiritual, as of people who, if they wore the cares of life, to a small boy seemed to wear them lightly."

He commuted back and forth to Coker for awhile, and then gave it up altogether because of the "air of unreality and detachment from life" which he felt on the campus. He had a few poems published during those years and tried writing short stories, but for the most part he farmed. His wife bore him two sons and a daughter to join his two older daughters, and through the war years and the rest of the '40s they were together there in the big house in the pines.

Dabbs was then a middle-class, middle-aged farmer, making an adequate living raising cotton and tobacco on 175 acres of arable land around the swamps of the old plantation. Negro families lived in half a dozen tenant shacks scattered through the pines, and Dabbs was kindly and paternalistic toward them, but like almost all Southerners, he tended to take for granted the segregated society that prevailed. Not that he didn't have some misgivings about it—in about 1940 he wrote an article for *The Christian Century* entitled "Is a Christian Community Possible in the South?" and concluded that it was not possible because of white supremacy—but he was not inclined to do anything in particular about it. In 1944 he wrote a letter to a newspaper in Columbia, the state capital, protesting the legislature's attempt to avoid desegregation by repealing the state primary election law. What angered him, though, was not the immorality of depriving Negroes of a voice at the polls but the "execrable exhibit of bad manners" which the law's repeal, in his eyes, amounted to. "Stealing votes didn't bother me—it was something you expected—but this new move was a public insult. I thought it was inexcusable to steal from people in broad daylight and then insult them at the same time."

It was clear by then that change was coming, and when it finally surfaced Dabbs quickly gravitated to the side of integration. This is how he tells it:

> I came late to my concern about racial injustice, but when it first began to be an issue in the '40s, I was in a position of having decided the issue for myself almost ten years before, without knowing I'd decided it. When I was thirty-seven [the year his wife died], I became rather suddenly aware of the fact that I was a human being, fundamentally like any other human being. Life had pretty well stripped me of most of what I valued, and I saw that I didn't have much left but my basic humanity. I wasn't thinking about race then—it was no deep concern of mine—but when the race issue did arrive, I didn't have to solve it for myself. As far as I was concerned, Negroes were human beings just like everybody else, and should have the same rights. I had enough common sense to know they *didn't* have the same rights, and that something had to be done.
>
> I came to this realization intellectually at first, from a basic

feeling about human nature and not from any passionate sense of injustice. I'm not a crusader, I've never been an activist, never been attracted to demonstrations—it's just not my style. I see a very full place for the activist, but it's not my cup of tea. And it's held for me, this idea of an abiding force rather than a passionate feeling for justice, which can burn brightly and then wear you out and you quit.

I came into the civil-rights movement partly because I was tired already. Segregation seemed to me not so much an evil thing as a useless, foolish thing. Life is tragic enough, hard enough, and segregation is an unnecessary burden. Why make life any more difficult? I was trying to get out of the toils and shackles of segregation. I've had Negroes say to me after speeches, "We thank you for what you're doing for us," and my answer has always been, "Well now, don't overpraise me. I hope you get something out of it, but I'm also doing this for myself. I just don't like segregation. It's a burden, and I don't see any use carrying a burden you don't have to carry."

So I got involved, and I've gone about my business. People reacted against it, of course; some members of my family reacted against what I was saying, and many people in the county did. But except when I wrote letters to the local paper, I don't think they knew much about me. They'd jump on me about the letters, but the national magazine articles they wouldn't see. People would call me on the phone occasionally and cuss me out, or write me letters, but I've been very little bothered by it, and my children, when they went through the local schools, weren't particularly bothered either. I'd say for the most part we've been ignored. As one segregationist told a friend of mine, "Everybody knows Dabbs is a damn fool— why bother with him?"

He laughed at the recollection. While he was thumbing a big pinch of tobacco into the bowl of his pipe, I asked him why he had left the "outside world" and come back to the plantation.

I came back here to this old place because it was quiet. There used to be a flower garden back at the rear of the house, a violet bed, and you went across a little stone bridge over a stream and into the garden, and you could kneel down on the brick walk and pick violets, and this whole place seemed to me a place of perfect peace and order. Though I came back to the plantation I never recommended that anybody else do it. I have no desire in the world to carry on the plantation pattern. It's out of date and outmoded, long outmoded.

It's always been a curiosity to me how my grandfather, a young man of twenty, could build this house in 1860 and '61 and barely get it through before the war broke out, and he didn't see what was coming. Yet within five years the whole system which might reasonably support such a house as this was blasted and gone forever.

Anyhow, there hung about this place a quietness and peace and vague sense of humor, and I don't think the peace and order were entirely phony. So I maintain that I have a tremendous advantage over the typical liberal, in that when I fight for the future at least I've got a feeling for what it is I fight for: it's got to have a certain order and peace and humor, a certain quietness, and if it doesn't have this, I'm not going to fight for it. But the typical liberal is so far away from this older order that he's flailing his arms in the dark. He may turn up something—a revolution may turn up something—but you waste a lot of effort that way.

Dabbs was quiet for a moment, and I waited for him to pursue further the comparison of Northern and Southern liberals.

Northern liberals are much more typical of the modern world. Southern liberals are hardly liberals at all. The Northerner has become more individualistic, farther from the old world, but he's more against than for. The Southerner retains a sense of community—he's critical, but not willing to chuck the whole thing. My position comes from these surroundings —from complacent and assured plantation people, like my mother, and also from impatient and critical and dissatisfied people, like my father.

Southern liberals are really conservatives. Even the Negroes who go North keep coming back to their old homes. Why, in

the name of common sense, do they, if this is such a hell of
a place, as all the liberals say it is? Well, the point is that it
isn't that kind of place. The system has been wrong and un-
just, but somehow there have been virtues—many small, perhaps, maybe some great—woven into the system. The Southern emphasis on decency, kindness, manners and so on was
built partly because the Southerner didn't have the courage
and imagination to wipe out the injustice, so he just did what
he could to make it a little more human. He should have
wiped out the injustice—we're still trying to do that—but he
didn't do bad when he tried to make it human. He only did
bad when he thought he had corrected the whole thing.

Even then, Negroes had this sense of community in the
South, and that's one reason they come back. The Negro has
been pushed to the outskirts of the white community, but
he's always been there. There is no absolute abyss and chasm
between whites and Negroes; they move back and forth across
the lines. There has been an unholy purpose behind this
movement, true—the Negroes were the hired help, the cheap
labor. The motives which have supported this system are essentially selfish, but human beings are more complex than
the theorists think, and they have hammered some good out
of this proximity to one another.

This kind of talk can be easily misunderstood, and often
has been. It is also hard to attack. "One of my theories is,"
says Dabbs, "that the trouble with Southerners is that they
don't love the South enough. I praise it and condemn it at
the same time." So he has stood his ground between the redneck and the revolutionary, appealing to the best instincts
of both—and fully convincing neither. It may seem an out-
dated stance in the current climate of extremism, but it was
radical enough in the early '50s, when Dabbs entered the
Movement, and in fact it was pretty close to the philosophy
of the Movement itself in those days. It was—and is—the
philosophical base of integration: look past the differences
to the similarities among men, build on the best of the past,
cast off the myths of superiority and inferiority, say, with
Martin Luther King, "I have a dream."

That's where Dabbs was when he first got into it, and that's where he is today. He says, "I'm one of these liberals, don't you see—with all the weaknesses of liberals—who think we could change things, and maybe even improve them somewhat."

He joined the South Carolina Council on Human Relations, the Southern Regional Council affiliate, and in 1957 he was elected president of SRC, a post he held for six years. In 1956 and '57 he laid aside most of his farming responsibilities to write *The Southern Heritage,* and since then has spent most of his time writing and talking about race and the South. In *The Southern Heritage,* he systematically attacked the defenses of segregation one by one, placed in historical context the reasons why we had come to that state of affairs, and concluded with a glimpse at The Dream:

> I have felt for a long time that the heart of the white South was divided between the desire for justice and decency and the desire for continued privilege. Patrick Henry said long ago we knew we should free the slaves, but, alas, life was too pleasant. Such a division means the weakening of moral identity, the tendency of the one self to break in two. But our division may be more critical than this. Properly fearful of abstractions, we here by a violent abstraction break the unity of our life apart. We draw a cold line down through our hearts and call it segregation. . . . No wonder we are afraid of abstractions; we are dying of one.
>
> . . . . I wouldn't blur with these running comments what I consider the basic situation in the South: that through the processes of history and the grace of God we have been made one people, and that it is disastrous to talk and act as if we were two. If, on the contrary, we would play the game wholeheartedly together, if we would be our deepest selves, there is no telling what great age might develop in the South. For here we are, two originally dissimilar people fused by the fires of history, one already, but lacking yet the courage to accept the fact. . . .

I had read the book before I went to Rip Raps, and while he talked of the vices and virtues of the South I recalled that passage about dissimilar peoples fused by history. He went back to the kitchen to fetch some iced tea, and I looked about the room at the tools of his trade and the mementoes of his past. A Hermes Rocket portable typewriter sat on the desk in the corner, surrounded by stacks of papers. Bookcases lined the walls, and all of them were full. He was working on a book about Southern writers, and their works dominated the collection—Warren, Styron, McGill, Faulkner, Richard Wright, Langston Hughes, Allen Tate, Flannery O'Connor, Lillian Smith, Dykeman and Stokely, Ellison, Harry Caudill, Tom Clark, Eudora Welty, and a score of others.

In the little bit of wall space not taken by books were a Phi Beta Kappa certificate from the University of South Carolina, a brotherhood award from the National Conference of Christians and Jews, and proclamations naming him a Sagamore of the Wabash and a Kentucky Colonel. Above the mantle was a plaque from the Detroit NAACP, dated April 9, 1961, with these words on it:

> To James McBride Dabbs, in grateful recognition of his wise and dedicated efforts to unify the American people in their quest of the democratic ideal.

Just beneath the plaque hung two Confederate rifles, crossed in an X.

After he wrote *The Southern Heritage,* Dabbs was a fixture on the civil-rights scene. In addition to the presidency of the Southern Regional Council, he was active in Penn Community Services, the Beaufort, South Carolina, Quaker center (he was chairman of its board of directors), and in the Fellowship of Southern Churchmen, which he served as president for two years when it was reactivated as the Committee of Southern Churchmen in 1965. In the hierarchy of the Presbyterian Church, U.S., he was instrumental in the drafting of policy statements on social concerns, including one on civil disobedience, which the church's General Assembly eventually adopted, and he has also been influential in tempering the rigid conservatism of the church. There is irony in that: though he is a ruling elder (a lifetime post) in Salem Presbyterian Church, a hauntingly beautiful, 123-year-old structure about a mile from the house where he was born, his appointments to commissions of the larger church were never the result of nomination by the local congregation. "I embarrassed them for awhile," he says, "and they didn't support me or defend me." Is he still active in the Salem congregation? "The only way they can get rid of me is bury me in the cemetery behind the church."

All of the Negroes who once lived on the Dabbs plantation are gone except a woman and her family who divide their time between there and New York, and two elderly men. The ones who remain are, with Dabbs, still at least partially bound by the old system of benevolent paternalism. He does not defend it, but for the older generation he is resigned to the inevitability of it as far as his own responsibility is concerned:

> Paternalism cut both ways. There was a time when the Negroes liked it too. The system is now in disrepute, and it should be, but Negroes as well as whites often find it hard to turn loose. There is the desire to be free, but there is also the need to have someone to depend upon. I used to tell my wife, "If I understood completely the relationship between my family and the family that lives at the head of the avenue [his name for the lane leading to the highway], I'd understand the whole South, the whole paternalistic system." Everybody was taking care of everybody else, and that "taking care of" could mean everything from real Christian compassion to the rough white man who said, "Leave them to me—I'll take care of them." This is fundamental in the South, something that marks Southern society. People *are* concerned—maybe sometimes for ill—but they're concerned about other people. It's on this particular ground that maybe we can make advances the rest of the nation can't make. In the rest of the nation, whites and Negroes have only recently been at all concerned

about one another, but down here, no man can do anything
without thinking what effect it will have on the other race.
This has evil in it, but also good. We are concerned across
racial lines.

But the fatal flaw, the unwillingness to purge itself of
the phlegm of white supremacy, has kept the South from
making those advances the rest of the nation can't make.
"There's been a tremendous change, in some ways, from the
South that said 'Never!' " Dabbs says, "but much of it has
been pragmatic change, an admission that open resistance is
hopeless. Change of heart, what religious people call conversion, comes much slower."

Does that mean racism has won, that integration is dead
and separation is the wave of the future? Does it mean the
South is simply a generation behind the North, bound in-
evitably to repeat its mistakes and add them to its own, to
undergo the same industrialization and depersonalization
and loss of community? Dabbs doesn't concede that:

> We're the most different Americans in America. There's
> more human nature in the South than anywhere else in this
> country. This doesn't sit well with a machined civilization. If
> we machine and industrialize and urbanize the South com-
> pletely, then you'll have to iron out most of the idiosyn-
> crasies and peculiarities, and there won't be much room for
> damn fools like Dabbs, because they cause too much trouble.
> But these changes are coming—they can't be stopped—and
> the question is whether we can assimilate them without giv-
> ing up altogether the assets that are our potential advantage
> in solving the racial issue.
> I sympathize with the white segregationist in the situation
> he's in. In some ways he is a more pitiful figure than the Ne-
> gro. Power has corrupted us, and the average Southern white
> racist is in an identity crisis. In the last one hundred years
> he's learned two things: you can't keep the Yankees out, and
> you can't keep the Negroes down. Faulkner says the South-
> erner is a man who resists. Well, if he can't keep the Yankees
> out or the Negroes down, then who is he? He doesn't know.
> There's nothing left for him to identify himself with. A man

in this emotional world is trapped. The white segregationist is more bound by the whole racial complex than the Negro, he's more frightened. At least the Negro knows what's got him—the white man's got him. But when the white man gets trouble, he doesn't know what's got him, and he's got himself all tied up.

I also sympathize with the Negro drift toward the black nationalist point of view. In the first place, he's been promised so many things, and we haven't delivered the promises. He thought he had a promise in the civil-rights movement, but it didn't amount to much. What good does it do him to be able to eat at Howard Johnson's if he hasn't got the job to have the money to eat there? I think I understand the forces that push him. So far as black awareness goes, this is a strategy. Negroes need to become aware of themselves, of who they are. If they join together politically and economically, they have much more power than they have individually, and can do much more. But if it's carried further than this, to the idea of setting up a separate Negro nation in certain states, that seems to me an utter absurdity. Even if they could do it they couldn't maintain it, because the modern world is built not upon separation but upon cohesiveness and interdependence. Trying to build a separate world now is simply trying to fight history. In the long run it's nonsense, but as a strategy, black power does have value for the present.

He had conceded nothing to racism. He went on to talk about violence, particularly violence rooted to slavery, and then came back to the black power theme to reinforce his defense of the South and its possibilities.

America is violent compared to Europe, and the South is violent compared to the rest of the nation. When we built our life upon slavery, we built upon violence, no matter how much the gloved hand tried to smooth it over. You arrested people, you captured people and you held people down, finally by force. This society was built upon violence, and therefore when violence erupts in man-to-man relationships, across racial lines or within the races, I don't think this is surprising.

Much of the violence among Negroes is due to the repres-

sion under which they've been held. There are two white
Southern myths that contradict themselves. One is, "These
are childlike people." The other is, "These are violent animals." Of course, the myths just eat one another up, but that
never bothered the Southerner; if two myths didn't agree, he
just created another myth. He's a great man for creating
myths. Violence among Negroes has often resulted because
he was compressed into close quarters—physical and psychological. Violence among poor whites has also resulted from
repression, from being controlled, from getting the short end
of the stick. All the people who controlled power would give
him was, "You're better than the Negro," and the destruction of that myth has left him bitter.

We developed a militia early because of slavery, and we
built a myth of feudalism, and feudalism meant an army—
the plantations were the castles. It is in these beginnings that
violence is rooted, the key factor being the oppression of the
Negro.

So the society was built upon violence. But ironically, in
spite of all our sins and errors, we still have the potentially
saving grace of community. Black power is not as strong in
the South as in the North, and I don't think it ever will be.
This, of course, is what the liberal theory doesn't take regard
of. Slavery was damnable, of course it was, but if you think
it was *just* this, you don't know human nature. People
devise some kind of way to live. According to the liberal
theory, the South is all wrong, everything is bad, you've got
to wipe it out, and this is what the more extreme black power
people are tending to say about white America. I don't think
it's true of America, and it's certainly not true of the South.

Negroes in the South who become engaged in extreme
movements such as black separatism face another problem, I
think. If they'll be honest with themselves, they'll find they're
not Negroes, period, or blacks, period—they're black Southerners. At root, it isn't blacks *against* whites, it's blacks *with*
whites. If we can have the courage and imagination to accept
this, then at least we'll be on the way to solving our problems. Finally we've got to admit that we're really one culture
—divided now by unfair practices and discrimination, but
basically one culture.

We had been talking for about three hours, but Dabbs showed no sign of fatigue. He is a vigorous man, big (six-feet-two, 190 pounds), and strong of voice, with wavy hair a shade of silver that suggests it was once straw blond, and a white mustache. It was late afternoon by now, and the sun was well down into the pines, but he had made the point about one culture, and wanted to pursue it.

I think this is perhaps the main thing I have to say. If I'm wrong, it'll all be forgotten, but if I'm right, then remember that I said it, because I've said it longer than anybody else I know of. It's this: Southern whites and Negroes are much more alike than they think. I really don't bother much about their *liking* one another—the more fundamental fact is that they are *alike* one another, and I think people who are alike just naturally come to like each other.

When Negroes first started joining the NAACP, the whites down here said, with some sincerity, "They shouldn't have done that. If they'd have come to me we'd have settled this thing. Why did they do this?" And Negroes have said to me, when whites took some obstructive position, "Why did the white people do that? They should have known better." These are first cousins talking about one another, don't you see, cultural first cousins. "Why should they have known better?" I would ask. "Because they were all brought up down here." In many of our attitudes in the South, the assumption is that whites and Negroes belong to the same group, and each one should understand the other. We grew up together, and this is the basic thing that strikes me about the South, that whites and Negroes are very deeply alike.

Take the first Negro students in the sit-in movement, in Richmond and Greensboro and across the South. Many of them were deeply, religiously dedicated. They weren't carrying the Bible just for show. There was a religious motivation, and that's typical of the South. We're still verbally a religious people. Whether it's deeper than verbal or not is another question, but we're religious—even the Ku Klux Klan has to have a chaplain. And the Negroes were being Southern when they were taking this action of commitment to principle. They showed a great sense of reserve, a true sense of manners.

They were challenging racial etiquette, but they were certainly doing it most decently.

James Kilpatrick, writing in the Richmond *News-Leader,* even broke into Latin way back then—that was 1960—to express his dismay. He said, *"Eheu"*—which means Alas, if I remember my Latin—*"Eheu,* that I should ever see Negroes teaching manners to whites." And I thought to myself, "Where has Kilpatrick been? Who taught whom the manners of the South anyhow?" The Negroes had as big a hand in it as the whites. I looked at the sit-inners and I learned something: these people are Southerners. Martin Luther King was one of the best Southerners we ever had, and I've been struck by the sense of humor, the lack of bitterness, the good clear minds and the level-headedness of Negro leaders in the South.

Anyway, these young people were Southerners. They had a deep commitment and a great reserve and a great quietness. Not many people recognized them as Southerners; in the first place, they didn't want to think of themselves as Southerners, because the Southerner was the white man, and they were rebelling against the white man's attitudes. And the whites didn't think of them as Southerners—they called them "outside agitators." But my contention is that they had picked up two of the basic attitudes of the South that for the most part the South had not been able to combine, and they had combined them: culture and religion, the surface of life with the inner thrust of life, the outside with the inside, a great and solid integrity with ease and calm of manner.

Restraint, manners, resiliency, commitment—this was the Southern ideal. We never had a chance of getting it, because we split ourselves by putting slavery at the bottom of the whole structure. But these young students in 1960 came about as close to getting it as any group of Southerners has ever come.

Not long after the sit-ins began, Dabbs was writing *Who Speaks for the South?* In it, he said this:

> . . . when it comes to defeat, Southerners, Negro and white, have resources not available to other Americans. In the experience of defeat, Negroes are our equals, perhaps our

superiors; certainly, they have been able to make better use of defeat than we have. If the whites of the South could realize and accept their defeat as a mark of their humanity, an indication of their participation in the common human doom, they would see all about them the faces of Negroes who had also participated, even more deeply, in that doom, and they would turn to them, as men in distress always turn to their fellows, seeking the outstretched hand. . . .

. . . A despised minority, excluded from the common life, returns at last more in love than in hatred to reveal to the majority, not only that possibility of community that has always haunted the mind of the South, but also and far more importantly a vision of the universal meaning of failure and defeat, revealing how men become human through the positive acceptance and affirmation of defeat. The man who was once servant reveals through his suffering to the man who was once master the meaning of suffering, and in this common realization paternalism breaks down and a democracy richer than we have ever known may arise.

It is the theme of The Dream, and more; he is not just talking about integration and equality and justice, he is talking about the Southern Negro as the key to it all, the one who unlocks the prison door and leads everybody, black and white, to freedom. And he is talking about the Southern white as the one whose experience shows him first that he is captive in his own prison.

Some say The Dream died with Dr. King, that non-violence has failed, that all the patience is spent, and there is no redemption. Others say the dream was a nightmare, a false promise that has spawned violence. These enemies face each other, their hatred not always under control, vowing that only the strong will survive the fire next time. And there is Dabbs, and the tattered remnant of Southern liberals, standing in the middle, praising the South and condemning it, calling it to look once again at the vision of what it could be.

Mrs. Dabbs came out to tell me good-bye—she had been

canning vegetables all afternoon—and then Dabbs walked with me out to the car. As I drove back up the avenue through that tunnel in the pines, I looked back at the great old house in the rear-view mirror. Dabbs had not tried to restore or preserve its ante-bellum character—or, for that matter, to disguise it. He had simply left it alone. Just as it is, it gives him what he wants: a quietness and peace, and a vague sense of humor.

John Lewis

> Some men see things as they are
> and say why. I dream things that
> never were and say why not.

George Bernard Shaw wrote that, and Robert F. Kennedy
was making it the theme of his campaign for the Presidency
when he was killed. It is a nice statement, full of idealism
and hope. It appeals to a lot of people who believe in the
principles and promises of American democracy—and who
have had few personal experiences to shake that belief. For
many people whose homes have been shattered, whose
churches have been burned, whose votes have been stolen,
whose heads have been broken—for many of America's dis-
inherited—dreams are nightmares, dreaded, dangerous, destructive things. For those people, hope is a luxury. The
reality is hopelessness and despair and rage.

But then there are people like John Lewis. He is a black
Southerner, thirty years old. He has fought for justice for
black people ever since he got out of high school in Pike
County, Alabama, in 1957. He has been to jail forty times.
He has been beaten unconscious in the streets.

George Bernard Shaw's idealistic credo hangs over the
sofa in John Lewis's living room. It is an affirmation of hope

that speaks to him. He likes it, and he believes deeply in the spirit of it. Dreaming things that never were and saying why not is pretty much what John Lewis has been doing for the past decade.

Lewis is an enigma. I heard a man who has known him for several years ask, "How could anybody who's been through what that guy's been through really be that free of bitterness and hate?" It's a good question. He has made a habit of doing unpopular things because he thought they were right, and he has paid a heavy price for it. Nonviolence brought down the wrath of white supremacy on his head—and later, it cost him his leadership role in the student wing of the civil-rights movement. He led marches and demonstrations when some of the most radical strategists of the Movement begged him to hold off—and he compromised when some of the same people counseled him to stand his ground. He followed his own social interpretation of the Gospel and left his church for the streets—just when a lot of "liberal" churchmen were hiding behind their stained glass windows. After both religion and politics had betrayed the black American masses, Lewis was able to bring innocent enthusiasm to a political cause. He has been denounced as a dangerous radical by the white Establishment—and some black radicals have written him off as not "black" enough, or not violent enough.

And John Lewis goes on being who he is—a gentle man, quiet and shy, as consistent and as persistent in his pursuit of justice for Negroes and the poor as he ever was. He is now director of the Voter Education Project of the Southern Regional Council in Atlanta. Four years ago, after he had lost the chairmanship of the Student Nonviolent Coordinating Committee to Stokely Carmichael, Lewis went to New York to work for the Field Foundation. He lasted fourteen months, and then gave it up and went South again—to stay.

The civil-rights movement led Lewis into the ministry—

and later out of it. He was born in 1940, six miles from Troy, Alabama, on a small farm his father rented. John was the third of ten children. In 1944 his father bought 100 acres of land in Pike County for $300, and it took the whole family to scrape out a living from the cotton, peanuts and corn they grew on it. School for them was a luxury—neither of his parents was able to go beyond the ninth grade—and there were times when John had to hide under the house and wait for the school bus, to keep from having to go to the fields.

As a teenager, one of his responsibilities was taking care of the chickens. "I fell in love with them," he recalls. "They were so innocent. I named them, talked to them, assigned them to coops and guided them in every night, and when one of them died, I preached his funeral and then buried him. I also protested whenever one of them was killed for food. I refused to eat." He smiled at the recollection. "I guess that was my first protest demonstration."

John wanted to be a minister, and that pleased his good Baptist parents, because there were no preachers in the family. But his interest in the ministry did not fit any traditional pattern. In Montgomery, fifty miles from his home, black people led by the Rev. Martin Luther King Jr. were boycotting the city buses, and Lewis was impressed: "It had a tremendous impact on me. I had come to resent segregation and discrimination at an early age. We had the poor schools, the run-down school buses, the unpaved roads; and I saw that those were penalties imposed on us because of race. So race was closely tied to my decision to be a minister. I thought religion could be something meaningful, and I wanted to use the emotional energy of the black church to end segregation and gain freedom for black people." He was ordained in 1956, the year before he graduated from high school.

Morehouse was where he wanted to go to college, but he didn't have the money. His mother worked for a white

Southern Baptist, and one day she brought home a magazine that had something in it about the American Baptist Theological Seminary in Nashville. ABTS was a small institution owned jointly by the National Baptist Convention (Negro) and the Southern Baptist Convention (white), with the latter group providing most of the support—a kind of insurance against desegregation. Lewis wrote for an application, filled it out and was accepted. He got a job as a dishwasher in the school kitchen to pay his room and board.

For the first couple of years, John didn't venture far from the seminary campus, but his attitudes about the organized church and the civil-rights movement continued to change. "My first semester I was in church every Sunday," he says, "but by the second semester I had begun to drift away. It was a period of real doubt and change for me. I started to question for the first time the ritual, the ceremony, the creeds and beliefs of the church, and I began to identify more and more with the social aspects of Jesus' life." He also formed close friendships with two fellows students at the seminary who later were active with him in the civil-rights struggle—Bernard Lafayette and James Bevel.

When he went home for Christmas his freshman year, Lewis made application to enter Troy State College as a transfer student, but his application was ignored. The Montgomery Improvement Association, headed by Martin Luther King, wanted to pursue the application in court, and John later met with King, Ralph Abernathy, and Fred Gray to discuss it, but his parents were afraid of the possible repercussions, so the matter was dropped. John also tried to organize a student chapter of the NAACP at the seminary, but the president feared losing Southern Baptist support, and once again he acquiesced.

By the fall of 1959, the South was beginning to feel the pinch of racial protest. School desegregation was the big issue—highlighted by the Little Rock episode—but other grievances were growing, and Nashville was a fertile field for some of them. Nashville's Negro colleges and churches had in their ranks a goodly number of black ministers, educators and students who became prominent in civil rights during the early 1960s. Although they and the black lawyers and the assortment of whites allied to the cause never joined together in any single organization, the city had a cadre of black leaders as diverse and talented as any city in the South. The NAACP, the new Southern Christian Leadership Conference headed by Dr. King, the Southern Regional Council, and other civil-rights groups had strong chapters there, and students from the city's colleges and universities were meeting and organizing before Atlanta and other cities got into the act. Young people such as Lewis, Bevel, Lafayette, the Rev. James Lawson, Diane Nash, and Marion Barry made the Nashville movement prominent as a center of young black protest.

Lawson, a Methodist minister and a student at the Vanderbilt Divinity School, conducted workshops in nonviolence for Nashville's SCLC chapter in the fall of 1959, and most of his students were young people from the colleges. Lawson lectured them on the philosophy, history, and discipline of nonviolence, and in November they staged the first sit-in in the South—three months before students in Greensboro, North Carolina, got national publicity using the same tactics. The Nashville sit-in was a test to establish the fact that lunch counters in the downtown stores wouldn't serve Negroes. The students requested service, were refused, and left. It all happened almost without notice, but it was the beginning, and after that there was no turning back. Lawson was later expelled from Vanderbilt Divinity School for leading the sit-ins.

The next month, on their way home for Christmas, Lewis and Lafayette boarded a bus for Birmingham, and took the front seat. The driver told them to move but they refused, and they rode all the way to Birmingham sitting there—two black youngsters full of pride and exhilaration at what

they sensed was happening to them and the movement and
the South. Lewis recalls the high spirits of those early
months:

> It was an exciting time, that time of beginning. Everything
> was so simple, and we were so clear about where we were
> going. It was just right. It was nonviolent, and interracial,
> and daring, and religious. It was like a holy war, a crusade,
> and we saw the movement rising across the South, we saw
> change coming, and we were helping to bring it about. We
> were volunteers committed to the philosophy of nonviolence,
> in keeping with the New Testament and the Christian faith.
> My motivation came from religious conviction—segregation
> was immoral, illegal and unchristian, and it had to be de-
> stroyed. You felt you had to be consistent with the truth, be
> faithful unto death, and there was integrity in that, and
> peace. Later, when we were charged with disorderly conduct
> and trespassing, we believed that a positive peace would
> come out of conflict, that it was a good thing to bring a lot
> of dirt and filth and trouble to the surface so it could be
> expelled.

Through the first six months of 1960, the sit-ins grew in
size and frequency. They were marked by victories and setbacks, new allies and new enemies, capitulations and hold-
outs, occasional violence and frequent arrest. Lewis was
arrested for the first time in February:

> We had been marching from Kelly Miller Smith's First
> Baptist Church, sometimes 200 or 300 of us at a time, but that
> day there were only thirty or so. Will Campbell told us that
> the merchants had been to the mayor and the police, and
> that we would surely be arrested if we marched. There was
> a real debate among the older leaders. Most of them didn't
> want us to go, but we went anyway. We had been well pre-
> pared in nonviolence—don't strike back, be polite, smile, be
> friendly, remember the teachings of Jesus, Gandhi, Martin
> Luther King—so we went. All of us were arrested, and we
> spent the day in jail. We went in high spirits, singing—we
> knew we were right. Bail money was sent in from the Na-

tional Student Association, and that was the start of the legal end of things—arrests, bail, trials, appeals, lawyers.

For Lewis, that process would be repeated many times.

In April, SCLC called a meeting in Raleigh for leaders of the sit-in movement, and students came from all over the South. King was there, and Ralph Abernathy, and Ella Baker, then the executive director of SCLC. "Some people wanted to form a student wing of SCLC," Lewis recalls,

> but the students wanted an independent organization. We formed a temporary independent group, with Marion Barry as chairman, and that was the beginning of the Student Nonviolent Coordinating Committee. The Atlanta and Nashville students were at odds with each other over where to put the headquarters. We had the best organized, best disciplined group, but they had the money, and SCLC offered to provide space, so the headquarters was set up in Atlanta, but we had the chairman in Nashville, and our student movement there remained the strongest for a long time.

Lewis says that Ella Baker, "perhaps more than any other person, was responsible for making SNCC what it became. She was sort of the mother of SNCC. She's a great lady."

With representatives from all the major civil-rights organizations there as observers, SNCC met in Atlanta the following October and formed a permanent organization. Barry was installed as chairman, and Diane Nash represented the Nashville chapter on the coordinating committee. More demonstrations followed in the winter and spring of 1961.

Then came the Freedom Rides. The Congress on Racial Equality sent out a call for volunteers to test a recent Supreme Court decision outlawing discrimination in interstate travel, and Lewis applied to go. After an orientation in Washington, he and twelve others set out by bus on two separate itineraries to New Orleans, with layovers and rallies planned at several places along the way. Lewis and his group rode buses through Virginia and North Carolina without encountering any serious incidents, but at Rock Hill, South Carolina, as they started toward the white waiting room, John was attacked and knocked down by a group of white teenagers. He got up, shaken but unhurt, and went on into the waiting room. A layover had been planned at a college in Rock Hill, and while they were there Lewis was called back to Washington for a meeting. He left the riders, and then made arrangements to stop in Nashville and finish his final exams at the seminary before rejoining the ride in Montgomery. In the meantime, a bus on which the other group of riders was traveling was burned outside of Anniston, Alabama, and violence broke out in Birmingham. By the time Lewis got to Nashville, the SNCC leaders there were trying to get more volunteers to take up the ride in Birmingham, but there was a strong feeling in the older civil-rights groups that the rides shouldn't continue, and then CORE decided to withdraw its sponsorship of them. "The Nashville Christian Leadership Conference had the money to finance some more riders," Lewis recalls, "and we met with them until the early morning hours, begging for support. They said it was suicide, but we kept after them, and finally they agreed to put up the money for ten riders."

On the morning of May 17, the ten—including three girls—boarded a bus for Birmingham, with Lewis as their spokesman. On the outskirts of Birmingham, he remembers,

the bus was stopped by city police, and two guys in our group who were sitting closest to the front were arrested and taken away in a patrol car. When we got to the bus station, we weren't allowed to get off. Finally they led us into the waiting room, and after awhile Bull Connor and the mayor came, and we were taken into protective custody, as they called it. The Rev. Fred Shuttlesworth tried to get us released, and they arrested him too. We all went to jail—it was Wednesday afternoon by then—and we went on a hunger strike. In the early hours of Friday morning, Connor came in and offered to let us go if we'd promise not to continue the freedom ride, but we refused, so they picked us up and

carried us to a limousine. There were seven of us by then—
the two guys who had been taken off the bus were later released, and one girl had got away before we were arrested.
Connor and his men started driving north, and he led us to
believe he was going to take us all the way to Nashville, but
when we got to Ardmore, right on the Tennessee line, at
about 4 A.M., he put us out on the highway and told us to
make it the best way we could.

After walking a short distance in the darkness, they saw
a little shack near a railroad crossing. Assuming—correctly,
as it turned out—that Negroes lived there, they knocked
on the door and finally roused an old man. He had heard
about the trouble, and when he found out who they were
he was reluctant to let them in, but finally he did. Lewis
called Diane Nash and learned that ten more volunteers had
been sent to take up the ride; he asked her to send a car to
pick them up so they could go back, too. While they were
waiting for the car, the old man went out for bread and
milk and bologna, and they ate for the first time in three
days.

The riders assembled later that day at Shuttlesworth's
house in Birmingham, and then went to the station and
waited for a bus to Montgomery. There was a large press
contingent there, and when dark came a mob gathered outside the station. The riders waited inside all night, but no
buses ran. Early the next morning they were able to board
one, and at last they set out for the Alabama capital:

All along the way we saw state troopers, and small planes
kept flying overhead. When we got into the station at Montgomery, there was nobody around, even though it was about
ten o'clock in the morning. It was so quiet, kind of eerie. We
stepped off the bus, and suddenly this angry, vicious mob
started coming from all directions. They attacked the press,
the girls, everybody. We finally got all the young ladies into
a cab, but the driver was black, and he wouldn't move because two of the young ladies were white and it was against
the law for a black cab to transport a white person. John

Siegenthaler from the Justice Department was there, and he got between the mob and the girls somehow and got them into a church, but Siegenthaler was beaten. All of us were beaten, and left lying in the street. I don't know how long I was unconscious—I was hit over the head with a heavy object. All our suitcases and belongings were thrown into a pile and burned. It was pretty bad.

Just how bad it was is difficult to comprehend. More than a score of people, most of them freedom riders, were injured, and violence spread through the city and continued sporadically for several days. The National Guard was called out, U.S. Marshals were sent in. The next day a mass meeting was held in Rev. Abernathy's church, and more mobs came. A smoke bomb was thrown into the church, and Governor John Patterson put the city under martial law and 1,200 people who were crammed into the church had to stay there through the night. Even after daylight came, it still took armed guardsmen to escort the people away from the church to safety. And in all that, press reports indicated that no instances of retaliation were discovered. The violence was all on the side of the white mobs.

Two days later, about forty freedom riders—Lewis among them—called a press conference to say they were going to Mississippi. They boarded two buses headed for Jackson, and rode with National Guard protection to the state line, where the Mississippi guard took over and escorted them the rest of the way. At the bus station all of the riders were arrested and taken to jail. They were run through a speedy trial, sentenced to sixty days, taken to the county prison farm—where some of them were beaten—and then to the Hinds County jail. At two o'clock one morning, they were taken out and moved to the state penitentiary at Parchman, 150 miles away. Lewis describes that experience:

It was a very frightening thing. I have never been more afraid in my life. They put the forty of us in a van, blacks and whites together—we had been segregated in our cells—

and drove us to Parchman in the dark of night. The guards kept their guns drawn all the time, and they taunted us, told us we'd be killed when we got there. At Parchman we were forced to strip naked and wait for an hour and a half, without knowing what was going to happen to us. It was very dehumanizing. For the first time in my life, I was literally afraid, terrified. They herded us into cells, still naked, with guns pointed at our heads, and we waited another two hours. Then they forced us to take showers and to shave all beards and mustaches, and we were given a pair of green shorts and a t-shirt, and those were the only clothes we got for the thirty days we were there.

After spending thirty-seven days under arrest, the riders were taken back to Jackson and released. John Lewis caught a train for Nashville:

My family never understood why I had become involved in all that. They had great fear of what it would all lead to, and they thought I was just going bad—getting in trouble with the law, going to jail and all that. I had lost any desire to be a preacher by then, and of course that troubled them too. So Nashville had become home for me. I did go back to Alabama to see my folks for a few days later that summer, but I needed contact with people who understood and supported me, and I couldn't get that kind of moral support at home. The Movement people became my family.

That fall, John enrolled at Fisk University in Nashville to work for a degree in philosophy—he had been graduated in absentia from the American Baptist Theological Seminary, while he was on the freedom ride—and he was elected head of the Nashville Student Movement and made a member of SNCC's executive committee. For the next two years he continued to lead demonstrations for SNCC—in Nashville when school was going on, and in such places as Cairo, Illinois, and Charleston, Missouri, in the summers.

By the summer of 1963, discrimination was being challenged in dozens of locations across the South, and the philosophy of nonviolent resistance dominated most of those challenges. In Birmingham, Dr. King and hundreds of other Negroes went to jail, and police used high-pressure fire hoses and police dogs in a vain effort to repress a sustained protest against segregation; in Jackson, NAACP Field Secretary Medgar W. Evers was slain from ambush outside his home after leading a campaign to abolish segregation in the Mississippi capital; at the University of Alabama, the National Guard had to be federalized to make Governor George Wallace end his "stand in the schoolhouse door" and let two Negro students enroll. In the midst of these developments, SNCC held a meeting in Atlanta, and John Lewis became the new chairman. He left Fisk lacking only a few hours to complete his degree, and moved to Atlanta to begin his year in office.

As chairman of SNCC, Lewis joined with the leaders of the other major civil rights organizations to plan the March on Washington. Looking back on it, that demonstration appears as the high-water mark of the nonviolent era. It brought the diverse elements of the civil-rights movement together for one massive show of unity, even as cracks were beginning to form beneath the surface. In his speech to the more than 200,000 people gathered at the Lincoln Memorial that August day, Lewis came off as the movement's angry young black man; his words were blunt and specific, in contrast to the more measured and less militant remarks of the "old guard"—Roy Wilkins, A. Philip Randolph, Whitney Young, and Martin Luther King. Even so, Lewis's remarks had been toned down the night before. He recalls:

> I had written the speech in Atlanta, and I felt it was representative of the feelings of the people in SNCC and those we were working with. The day before the march, copies of all the speeches were distributed to the press, and that night, Bayard Rustin called me to a meeting to discuss it. I was told that Archbishop Patrick O'Boyle wouldn't give the invocation unless I changed my statement. In it, I had said we

couldn't endorse President Kennedy's civil-rights bill—it was too little, too late—and I had said we couldn't be patient any longer, and I had said we would march through the South like Sherman did and burn Jim Crow to the ground—non-violently—and they were upset by all that. Mr. Randolph supported me on some of the points, but he said that for the sake of unity I should change the speech, so I did.

It was still a tough speech. Dr. King's famous "I have a dream" oration aspired to a future world of brotherhood; John Lewis's demanded "freedom now." But many of Lewis's compatriots in SNCC were disturbed and bitter that he had altered the speech, and many of the fractures which later spread through the Movement were already beginning in the student ranks. Paul Good, writing four years later in the *New York Times Magazine,* described the SNCC of mid-1963 as:

> an organization already in flux, its original Southern element stirred by Northern recruits. Bohemianism was rubbing shoulders with old-time religion; nonviolence was alternately a creed and a tactic. Black Southern youth who saw salvation in the right to vote heard disillusioning Northern tales of ghettos that generations of black ballots could not vote away. Lewis was the embodiment of a deep paradox. Here was a young man of rural courtliness and moral high-mindedness, a square even, leading a group that generally disdained bourgeois manners and morals as just another American hangup.

For the next three years, while Lewis was serving as SNCC's chairman, the organization was represented just about everywhere that a civil-rights issue was raised—in the Alabama black belt and the Mississippi delta, in Maryland and Virginia, in Washington and New York and Atlanta. Lewis himself went from voter-registration campaigns, sit-ins, and demonstrations to speaking and fund-raising trips, from the jailhouse to the White House, and in all that he maintained the same curious mixture of manners and militancy that had marked his style since his first involvement in 1959. Later he remarked to a friend: "I learned early to pace myself. I felt we were involved in a lifetime struggle —hard, tedious, continuous. There were disappointments, but I had faith that continued pressure and pushing would pay off. I was still religious, but not in the traditional sense. You have to have a sense of hope and perseverance. You have to have a sense of hope to survive. I didn't give up, I didn't become bitter or become engulfed in hatred. That's just not a part of me."

After President Kennedy was killed, the civil-rights heat got hotter, and it was harder to find a focus in the movement. The Mississippi Freedom Summer followed; Chaney, Goodman, and Schwerner were murdered; Congress passed the Civil Rights Act of 1964; the Johnson-Goldwater campaign prompted four civil-rights leaders—King, Wilkins, Young, and Randolph—to declare a moratorium on mass demonstrations until after the election. Lewis and James Farmer of CORE refused to join them. John didn't criticize the other organizations, but he felt that SNCC had its own role to play, and he kept at it in spite of complaints from the older organizations and from the radical wing of his own outfit. Lewis was on the SCLC board of directors, and he considered Martin Luther King his friend and his hero; he didn't hesitate to disagree with King, but he would not denounce him, and some of SNCC's left wing found it hard to accept such distinctions. There was Lewis, sticking to his belief in nonviolence, and to his support of white people in the movement, and to his friends in SCLC—his old schoolmates, James Bevel and Bernard Lafayette, were by then a part of King's team—and all of that clashed at times with the ideas and wishes of some other SNCC regulars, including James Forman, the executive secretary, and Stokely Carmichael, whose first trip south landed him in the pen at Parchman with the rest of the Freedom Riders.

Lewis won re-election to the chairmanship in 1964 and again in 1965. In 1964 he went to Africa on a trip arranged by Harry Belafonte, traveling with a group that included

Mrs. Fannie Lou Hamer, Julian Bond and Don Harris (his two closest friends in SNCC), Robert Moses, Jim Forman, and half a dozen others. Lewis and Harris traveled on alone to other parts of Africa after the group had stayed three weeks in Guinea as the guests of President Sekou Toure, and they were in Ethiopia when Johnson trounced Goldwater and Bobby Kennedy won a New York Senate seat.

Soon after he got back, the voter registration campaign was started in Selma, Alabama, and Lewis was among the first to be arrested there. Demonstrations went on there for more than two months, marked by some of the worst violence of the decade, and by the time the protracted demonstration was climaxed on the steps of the Alabama capitol in Montgomery after a march from Selma, at least three persons had been killed, scores injured (including Lewis, who was hospitalized after a beating by police), and hundreds jailed. And the speeches from the capitol steps that day sounded the same note of insistence and militant determination that had marked John Lewis's unedited statement at the March on Washington eighteen months before.

The Voting Rights Act of 1965 followed Selma. And Watts happened that summer, too—it was the first big explosion outside the South, and one of the growing number of signs that the civil-rights movement was undergoing rapid change. By the spring of 1966, Lewis had open opposition for re-election to the SNCC chairmanship:

> I had been to Norway and elsewhere in Europe on a speaking tour, and when I got back just before our annual meeting in Nashville, Stokely Carmichael told me he would be a candidate. I believe he had run in 1965—he and several others—but I had won. I guess I was the representative of the Southern nonviolent philosophy—the main reason I was ever elected in the first place was that the Nashville movement was so well organized, and each year after that the dominant faction was the one I represented: pro-South, pro-nonviolence, pro-SCLC, pro-interracial.
>
> We met for several days in May, at a retreat outside of

Nashville. The night of the election there were about 200
people there, including several ex-SNCC people and others as
observers. I was nominated for chairman, along with Stokely
and one or two others. The vote was taken and I won by a
large margin. Jim Forman had resigned as executive secretary, so Stokely was nominated for that post, but he declined.
The election was closed. But then one of the ex-SNCC guys
challenged the whole procedure, he challenged the election,
and a big argument started. It got around to my relationship
with Martin King, and my past contacts with the White
House, and before it was over it got very low and nasty. Some
people felt it was time for a change from nonviolence and
integration to something else. King was considered an Uncle
Tom, a sellout, white people were no longer wanted. It was a
bitter night. Finally, the election was held over—many of the
Southerners had left by then—and this time Stokely won by
a big margin.

Earlier, Lewis had decided he would resign at the meeting and not run for re-election, but he changed his mind and
stayed to fight it out. Part of his reason had to do with the
North-South split in the ranks:

> The Southern black students in SNCC had an altogether
> different outlook than the ones from the North. I don't know
> what it was exactly, but it always caused a tension, and it
> centered around nonviolence, and around how you react to
> people. The way it ended for me was a serious blow, a per-
> sonal thing, and it affected me very much. I saw the end of
> the beginning. I saw the death of SNCC, of the movement.
> We had had a diverse group, reaching into all parts of the
> country, it had all been very new and hopeful.

As things turned out, Lewis's vision of the end was very
nearly accurate. The following month, James Meredith
started his one-man "march against fear" through Mississippi
and was shot from ambush on the second day. Civil-rights
leaders and supporters flocked to the state to take up his
march, and Carmichael, with others, launched the "black
power" rallying cry at every stop along the way. Lewis was

there when the march reached Canton, and that night he spoke to the crowd. He talked about nonviolence, but it just wouldn't mix with the new mood: "I felt like an uninvited guest. It wasn't the same anymore, something was missing. I tried for a while to stay on in SNCC, but the position they were taking was inconsistent with my own convictions. Canton was the last scene for me. About a month later, I resigned from SNCC."

After that, Lewis went to work in New York for the Field Foundation, whose executive director, Leslie Dunbar, had formerly headed the Southern Regional Council in Atlanta. John didn't like New York; he missed the South, and after a little more than a year he went back to Atlanta to join the staff of SRC.

"You have to have a sense of hope to survive," he had said. Lewis's experiences could have made of him an underground guerrilla warrior, a true revolutionary. Instead, he emerged with as much faith, hope, and love as he had when it all started. Through something like double vision, he managed to see the good qualities in others—like John Kennedy and Lyndon Johnson—and his own imperfections, and that kind of vision makes only gentle revolutionaries.

Working in SRC's Community Organization Project with Al Ulmer, Lewis immersed himself again in the Southern struggle against discrimination and poverty. The headline figures had gone North, followed by the television cameras and the press corps. New civil-rights laws were on the books, and the issues had changed to Vietnam and the cities. It was quiet in Selma and Bogalusa and Americus. But for most blacks—and many poor whites—the necessities of food and shelter and employment and human dignity were as elusive as ever.

After John Kennedy was assassinated, Lewis gained a deeper respect and admiration for Bobby Kennedy than he had felt for him as attorney general: "I came to see him as the only political figure who could have bridged the gaps in this country and in the world, especially among the young and those who sought their freedom. There was something so basic, so good and passionate and understanding about him. He changed a lot after his brother was killed, he grew. The day he announced his candidacy for the Presidency in March 1968, I took leave from SRC and joined his campaign."

Lewis was with Kennedy in Indianapolis when Dr. King was assassinated. John was stunned by the news—his hero was dead—but he got another one that night: "Kennedy spoke at a rally after the news of Dr. King's death, and he did such a fine job, so sensitive, so fine. I saw his campaign then as an extension of the movement, as another step after the March on Washington, after Selma. Martin's death made it all the more important for me to work in Bobby's campaign, and I was able to transfer my loyalty to him."

From Indiana to Oregon to California, John worked as one of the RFK loyalists. The day before the California primary he witnessed

> a tremendous outpouring of public support for him, and I knew the guy had something going for him. After the election the next day, I was in his room at the Ambassador Hotel. We were sure he had the victory sewed up, and everybody was in high spirits. Bobby laughed and said to me jokingly, "You let me down, John. The Mexican-Americans turned out better than the blacks." And then he asked some of us to wait there while he went down to make the victory speech. We were watching on TV when it happened.

Bob Kennedy died, practically right before their eyes, and one more light went out for John Lewis. He wandered in a daze, down to the ballroom, then outside, then to the office Kennedy staffers had shared in a nearby hotel, then back to the Ambassador. Finally he stretched out on the floor somewhere and fell asleep, and then packed his bag and caught a plane for Atlanta. It was the end.

Or so it seemed. But the survival instinct prevailed, and hope returned. Later in the summer, Julian Bond led a challenge against the Georgia delegation to the Democratic Convention, and Lewis couldn't stay out of it. He went to Chicago with the Bond delegation, and cast his one-half vote for Teddy Kennedy. And when November came around, he couldn't bring himself to waste the first ballot he had ever cast in a Presidential election. He considered the choices pragmatically, and voted for Hubert Humphrey.

Lewis is married now. He and his wife, Lillian, live in Atlanta, and he still works for the Southern Regional Council. He goes back to Troy more often than he once did: "My family remains active in the church—my father is a deacon —and they more or less think I've lost my way, but I think they're coming to understand better what I've tried to say and do. We're closer now than in a long time. I've tried consciously not to separate myself from my family. I have a deep love for them, for the outdoors, for what I consider home."

Home is the South. Lewis says:

> I think in the South we've all been the victims of violence and brutality, both those who have suffered it and those who have practiced it. We've all lived in it. There's a degree of humanity about Southerners that's perhaps different from people elsewhere. There's an element of human understanding, of compassion, and we have that to build on simply because of what we've been through. It can become real. We can be more loving, more forgiving; we can more readily understand. We're going through a transitional period now, but I don't think it will be with us long. I have abiding faith that something good and positive will emerge. We can't continue on this level. All the violence, the wars, the riots, the assassinations, it's all too much. It will have to force the best out of us, the true good. I believe it.

There is no doubt that he does. John Lewis dreams things that never were, and says why not.

Howard (Buck) Kester

Meet a young radical: He spends his time and energy organizing students and workers. His bag is participatory democracy, democratic socialism. Communism, to him, is at best irrelevant and at worst a dangerous threat. His goals are peace, racial justice, and economic freedom for the masses. He is also a theological radical: his denomination dismissed him from a student pastorate, and he has been forced out of one seminary for his iconoclasm and denounced in another for organizing a student protest against Western military intervention in Asia. He is an embarrassment to his middle-class father. He has dabbled in politics, running for Congress as a Socialist. Still under thirty—if only by a few months—he is already a ten-year veteran of the struggle against the Establishment.

That description could fit some of the young revolutionaries in the Students for a Democratic Society, or in some other branch of the New Left. It also fits a guy named Buck Kester—that is, it did in 1934, before today's under-thirty generation was born. Howard Anderson Kester, now sixty-six years old, is alive and well, living in the mountains of western North Carolina. He is dean of students at a small junior college founded and operated by the Presbyterian

Church in the United States—the same body that dismissed him from the pulpit forty-five years ago.

Kester was the Eugene V. Debs of Dixie, he was Norman Thomas with a Southern drawl. His father was a merchant tailor from a Quaker family, a Presbyterian elder and a member of the Ku Klux Klan; his mother esteemed Robert E. Lee as her patron saint, "but apprehended the significance and meaning of Lincoln." They were Southerners—Virginians—and they were middle class, not by today's economic index but by comparison with the very rich and the very poor who were so conspicuous at the turn of the century, perhaps even more conspicuous than they have now come to be again. Howard was their third child, and their only radical. He was forty years before his time.

He roamed the South for four decades, crusading for racial and economic justice for the black and the poor, long after Reconstruction had betrayed and denied the Negro, after Populism had gone white and ugly and then impotent, after Jim Crow had established his barnyard rule, and before the civil-rights movement was born. It was a lonely, uncertain, and dangerous time for white men so inclined, almost as hazardous for them as for the Negroes who refused to accept white domination. Buck Kester was one of the few, a man radicalized by a vision of Christian brotherhood and by a land impervious to such notions.

His odyssey from Martinsville, Virginia, to Montreat, North Carolina, took him to all parts of the South, to New York, to Europe. He was at times, in fact or in spirit, a man without a church, without a home, without a country, a fugitive at large in Babylon.

We seem to have a way of assimilating radicals in this country. They are co-opted by the System, absorbed, popularized, institutionalized, prostituted, bastardized. Or they're pre-empted, replaced by a more radical wave or by a swing in the other direction. Some of that happened to Buck Kester. But Buck is a lot like Norman Thomas, whom he idolized; what Buck is after now is the same thing he was seeking in 1923, and the main reason he's not a radical any more is that a lot of people now speak out for racial justice, peace, and economic freedom for the masses. Saying those things is no longer radical. It is the skill—or the will—to make them happen that is lacking, and it is that lack which produces this generation's rebels.

I met Buck Kester in his office at Montreat-Anderson College on a cool, misty October day. He and his wife, Alice, live on the campus, and they have a mountain cottage at High Top Colony, a few miles away. We drove up there to spend the afternoon, passing close under the low clouds that clasped the mountains. The cottage is actually their "family" home, a roomy, comfortable place they built thirty years ago and have lived in, off and on, ever since. It sits snugly in deep woods on the mountainside, above a clear brook which crosses the road within sound of the front porch, and in autumn the forest floor around it is carpeted with leaves of amber, rust and scarlet. In the kitchen we opened a can of chicken à la king and brewed some tea, and then he told me the story of one radical growing up absorbed in the pre-civil-rights South.

The Kester family moved from Martinsville to Beckley, in neighboring West Virginia, when Howard was twelve years old, and five years later, in 1921, he went back to Virginia to enter Lynchburg College. He took with him "the characteristics of a Southern white boy, but not the deep prejudice." He had learned from his mother to be courteous and civil to all people, but a kind of benevolent paternalism, rather than any notion of equality, dominated what thoughts he had about Negroes. At the end of his sophomore year, he went with a group of fifteen boys on a trip to Europe sponsored by the World Student Christian Federation, and after they returned he was invited to the Lynchburg Theological Seminary and College, a Negro institution, to tell about the trip. "Channing Tobias was there," Kester recalls. "He was then secretary of colored work for the YMCA, and later was one of the first U.S. representatives to the United Nations, a wise, able, polished man. When I spoke in chapel, I tried to express understanding of the disadvantages of the Negro, and I used the word 'patience.' Instead of giving me a pat on the back when I got through, Tobias gave me the worst oral spanking I've ever had. 'Be patient?' he said. 'What do you think we've been?' His words forced me to some hard thinking."

That year, Howard and other students from his college and the theological school organized what he describes as "the first student interracial group in the South." They were a conspicuous and unpopular minority, "feeling that something was drastically wrong with the society around us and wanting to do something about it." Kester also became involved in a program to raise funds for European colleges and students in their post-war rehabilitation effort, and by the time he graduated from Lynchburg in 1925 he was a seasoned veteran of organization work in the South.

Howard wanted to be a preacher, but since his high school days he had been increasingly aware "of how unrelated the church was to society, to the whole process of living." He recalls the U.S. Army's First Division being sent to Beckley in 1919 to put down a miners' war: "The miners were on strike, and the army was supposed to get things under control. They weren't very successful, so the mine operators brought in Billy Sunday to break the strike. He preached on Americanism, and did what the army couldn't do. That sharpened my concern and my knowledge. I saw how removed and irrelevant the church was, how it was serving the interests of the privileged class."

Later, at about the same time he was helping to organize the student interracial group and working for European student relief, Kester was also serving as a student pastor at a Presbyterian church in the West Virginia coal fields. Again, there was a strike in the mines, and Howard, whose church members were miners and operators, felt that the church "should have something to say about this." His sympathies were clearly with the exploited miners, and when he began to work that into his sermons and to relate social problems to the Gospel, his days were numbered. "The man responsible for sending me to that church sent an elder over to hear me, and that's the last appointment I ever had in the Presbyterian Church."

In the fall of 1925, Kester went to Princeton Theological Seminary, and quickly became active in a small group of about twenty radical students—radical, at least, by Princeton's standards at that time:

> We weren't being challenged, we were getting nothing from the classroom, there was no interest in the social significance of education—all that seemed to matter was belief in the right dogmas and doctrines. Our little group was concerned about race, peace, and industry, and we took issue with segregation, with students who belonged to the Klan, with a professor who was on the lecture circuit defending child labor. Negroes were treated as nobodies. I went to a Negro church and learned that the pastor was the last Negro who had been allowed to attend the seminary as a regular student—after him, they could only get in as special day students. We talked to the president, whose name was Stevenson, and told him of our concerns—we were confused and disturbed, and we were looking for guidance. He was troubled by our problems and questions, but he was very understanding. Later he called me to his office to explain why I had not accepted the scholarship offered me when I had enrolled. I told him I was sure the donors of the funds hadn't given the money for the likes of me. By that time, our little group of twenty was down to three.
>
> When it came my turn to preach in chapel, I took the text the faculty had assigned to me—it was from John's Gospel, "What does it matter to thee, follow thou me." I regarded it as a challenge straight from the Almighty, and I talked about all the things on my mind—war, child labor, exploitation of

the poor, churchmen and the Klan, racism—and I was very specific at points, naming names. The chapel was packed, and some of the students were incensed. Their threat to throw me in the lake was thwarted by my two friends, Carter Swain and Bob Stewart, who slipped me out a side door. Later, Dr. Stevenson invited me to his home for dinner, and we talked long into the night. Finally he said, "Kester, you're rejecting eighteen centuries of Christian thought," and I guess he was right—I *did* question many of the tenets and practices of the organized church. I accepted the teachings of Jesus, *in toto*. We prayed together, and then I was up all night, worrying. By ten the next morning, I was on the train for home.

The interracial student group he had been active in at Lynchburg gradually became associated with the YMCA and YWCA, and the summer after his Princeton experience Kester went to a conference of the two Y's in North Carolina. There he met two people who were to have a profound influence on his life. One was a pretty Georgia coed named Alice Harris, who became his wife eight months later. The other was George Washington Carver.

Dr. Carver had been invited to speak at the conference, but no arrangements had been made for his meals and lodging, so Kester's crew from Lynchburg took him in as their guest. Some student delegations threatened to walk out if and when Carver spoke at the meeting, but the walkout never materialized.

That summer started a close friendship between Kester and the famous Tuskegee scientist, and when Howard went back home to Beckley after the conference, he had made up his mind to go to Tuskegee and spend the rest of the summer with Dr. Carver. His mother and his sister, who was eight years older than he, seemed to have some understanding of what drove Howard, though they thought he was far too radical. His father never understood at all: "My father's people were Quakers, and he had some remnants of Quakerism in him, but he had a volcanic temper, almost uncontrollable. He was an elder in the Presbyterian Church and a member of the Klan. When I told him I was going to Tuskegee, he said, 'If you go, don't ever come back.' So I packed my belongings in a trunk and took off. He later relented, and we were reconciled before he died in 1928."

In high school, Kester picked up the nickname "Buck" from a character in a Zane Grey novel, and the name stuck when he showed spunk as a hard-nosed little halfback on the college football team. It also seemed to fit his stubbornness and determination, traits he no doubt inherited from his father—and used as defenses against him when he cut the cord and went to Tuskegee. Buck went to Decatur to visit Alice Harris, and then spent a month under Carver's tutelage:

> He taught me about ferns, moss, herbs and other plant life, and a genuinely warm friendship grew up between us. He showed me his correspondence with Edison, we talked about starting a Carver fellowship to make religion manifest in the sciences, and he took me into his confidence as he did few people. After that, I saw him often, and we corresponded for years. I had over 300 letters from him. In all my moving about they have been lost, to my great sorrow, but I still have some of his paintings.

When he enrolled in the school of religion at Vanderbilt University that fall, Buck Kester was a notorious young man. At twenty-two, he had already been involved in enough controversies to spread his name. His reputation preceded him to Nashville, and he wasted no time living up to it. He was hired as associate secretary of the YMCA at Vanderbilt, and helped to form an interracial organization of students from Vanderbilt, Peabody, Fisk, Tennessee A & I, and Scarritt. That winter, he and Alice were married, and three weeks later he was fired from his job. He recalls the circumstances:

> The Western allies had just intervened in China, and our student group was incensed. I called a meeting on the Vander-

bilt campus, we had three missionaries in to speak, and we ended up firing off a cablegram to a group of Chinese students, telling them we supported them. Our little interracial meeting made the papers, and caused a furor. The dean publicly defended the French and British for the job they had done in Asia, and afterward he called me in and gave me hell. I was fired, and so was the secretary of the Y, and we were denounced by all the presidents of the Nashville colleges.

The Fellowship of Reconciliation, a religious, pacifist organization in New York, offered Howard a job, and he and Alice packed up and left Nashville. Two years later they came back, and Howard re-entered Vanderbilt and served at the same time as a one-man Southern staff for the Fellowship, a job he kept for five years. During that time he got his divinity degree, ran for Congress on the Socialist ticket (he got about 3,500 votes and finished second, ahead of the Republican candidate), attended an international pacifist convention in Europe, got involved in a miners' strike in the Tennessee mountains, and sought out Earl Browder, the leader of the American Communist Party, to find out for himself whether communism had anything to offer him. He concluded that it didn't.

Those were the depression years, and political nostrums for a sick society were heard everywhere. Kester tells how his meeting with Browder came about:

After a meeting in Chattanooga, five of us—including two Negroes—decided we wanted to find out more about this communism business—maybe there was something to it. So we went to New York and called Earl Browder on the telephone, told him we wanted to see him. He wouldn't let us come to his office, but invited us to his home. We talked for two hours, but it only took me fifteen minutes to know it was something I never wanted anything to do with, and the others felt the same way. It was Browder himself that convinced me—his duplicity, his disregard for morality and ethics. He was very frank about it: "This is the goal, and it doesn't matter what you do to achieve it." Not one of us joined; in fact, one of the fellows later helped to block a communist takeover in Italy. From then on, I fought them everywhere I went. I almost got sucked in once or twice, because their stated objectives were the same as mine—peace, race, industry. They called interracial conferences, set up front groups, tried to exploit racial division in the South. I went to one meeting in Birmingham and got named to the executive committee of one of those groups, but they made the mistake of letting me speak to the meeting, and I blasted communism from start to finish.

Kester could have been described as a Christian, anti-communist, democratic socialist. To a lot of people, he was splitting hairs; to him, the distinctions between his philosophy and that of the communist organizers were fundamental and crucial. He organized the Socialist Party in Nashville, and became closely associated with Norman Thomas: "I believed in Thomas and his ideas. I grew to esteem him, and I joined the party because of him, as did most of my friends." Kester ran for Congress the same year Franklin Roosevelt was elected. And over the years, his antipathy for communism increased.

The miners' strike also started in 1932, and for the better part of two years, Buck and his wife devoted most of their energies to helping the miners. It all started at Wilder, a coal-mining village on the Cumberland Plateau, about one hundred miles east of Nashville. After absorbing two reductions in wages, the union voted not to accept a third pay cut planned by the coal companies. The miners walked out, and the mines were idle for several months. "The miners were in an unimaginable plight," Kester recalls.

There were about five hundred families with no income. The companies tried starvation, they tried injunctions, they brought in the state militia, but they couldn't force those poor people to give in. Alice and I went to help the miners win their battle, taking them food and clothes which we got by organizing relief agencies in Nashville and elsewhere. Finally, in April of 1933, the companies brought in thugs from Illinois to break the strike, and they gunned down Barney Graham, the union leader, in the street at Wilder. Those people were making about $24 a month when the mines were open, they were in hock to the company store, but they wouldn't surrender. They had dignity and courage, they had frustrations and belly hunger, but they held on, and after Barney was killed their determination increased.

Kester's blue eyes brimmed with tears as he talked about the miners. He sat slumped in his chair, a short, slender man with a ruddy complexion and wavy, gray-black hair. Alice, sitting across the room, said nothing. Buck lit a filter cigarette, took off his glasses, rubbed his bushy white brows, and then chuckled, a quick, easy laugh. "We got them out," he said. "I went to Dr. Arthur Morgan of the TVA, and he got the Resettlement Administration to help move the families out to homesteads in Crossville. We did it, and in a few months a complete change came over them. People said if you gave those poor folks a bathtub they'd fill it with coal. Never was a lie so routed. They were new people. They rose. They blossomed."

Wherever Buck went, Alice was with him. Then in 1934, their only child, Nancy, was born in Nashville, and that same year Kester and the Fellowship of Reconciliation parted company:

> People in the peace movement always asked me how I could be a pacifist and be involved in the struggles of labor, where violence of some sort was almost a daily occurrence. (I never was a simon-pure pacifist, but I loathed violence of any sort.) My answer was that we were all involved in the class struggle whether we liked it or not. Consciously or unconsciously, we participated in the exploitation of workers even when we bought a ton of coal or a loaf of bread. We lived upon the hunger and the social wretchedness of the poor, black and

white. Many people in the Fellowship of Reconciliation couldn't understand this reasoning. I was particularly censured for allowing miners to guard me after company gunmen had promised to blow my brains out—and they almost succeeded in doing that.

A group within the Fellowship led by J. B. Matthews and Reinhold Niebuhr resigned over the issue of Kester's censure, and these people—Matthews, Niebuhr, Roger Baldwin, Elizabeth Gilman and others—formed the Committee on Economic and Racial Justice and set Kester free to work at whatever he thought important and urgent.

For the next seven years he moved around the South "doing his own thing," as a later generation would say. During that time he was ordained by the Congregational Church in a peculiar proceeding that took two days and involved about thirty-five churchmen in a monumental debate: "I was a New Testament Christian, and that was it. I had no great concern for the doctrines. My statement of faith was simply that the measure of a man was the way he lived in terms of others. I was accused of using religion as a cloak for my socialist interests, and there was strong opposition to my ordination, but after two days, all but three of the participants endorsed me. When it was over, Douglas Horton, general secretary of the Congregational Church, said the experience had been one of the most fruitful and educational of his life."

During those years, Kester also was instrumental in the organization of the Fellowship of Southern Churchmen, worked with the Southern Tenant Farmers Union, investigated lynchings in the South for the NAACP and the American Civil Liberties Union, lectured on scores of college campuses across the country, wrote a book—*Revolt Among the Sharecroppers*—and built the house at High Top Colony on the mountain across from Montreat. The book, now out of print, was his account of the activities and goals of the tenant farmers union; it has become a classic in the field of

Southern labor history. The investigations of labor unrest and lynchings took him all over the South, and often got him into serious trouble.

But it was with the union and the new churchmen's organization that he spent most of his time, and it was for just such things that the Niebuhr committee had hired him. He recalls:

I went to the Southern Tenant Farmers Union in Arkansas in 1935. It was the height of the campaign to organize sharecroppers all over the South, and the Arkansas group, though it had only a few hundred members, was a clear threat to racial segregation and to the economic exploitation of the poor. Here for the first time, Negro and white tenant farmers, sharecroppers and day laborers joined together to challenge their exploitation by the landowners.

Almost every meeting was broken up by the landowners or the law—they worked hand in hand. Our members would bring their guns—that was not illegal—and they would stack them in the meeting house, to be used if necessary. I was convinced that *not* using the weapons was our only hope, and that was not only a philosophical but a practical belief. H. L. Mitchell, the union leader, finally came to that conclusion too, and the members, black and white, adopted nonviolence as their guiding principle.

Mitchell had to move to Memphis from his home in Marked Tree, Arkansas, for the safety of his family. The intensity of hatred over the labor issue was so deep and profound, it's a wonder either of us is alive. I remember one night we all got out of the house where we were meeting after being tipped that a raid was coming, and in a little while several cars rolled up out front and sprayed the house with machine gun bullets. The wife and daughter of the man who owned the house were wounded, but all of us escaped. On another occasion, we were visited by Jennie Lee, a member of the British House of Commons and later the wife of Aneurin Bevan, the great British Labour Party leader. She and two other ladies wanted to see labor conditions in Arkansas, but we were told by the authorities that we couldn't have a meeting in our little union hall in Marked Tree. So we met on the Illinois Central railroad tracks—and then marched two by two down the main street to the union hall. There were cars loaded with armed men all along the street, but no trouble developed.

Then there was another close call. A plantation in Cross County evicted all its tenants in January, and they moved into tents set up around a Negro Baptist Church. The people were constantly threatened, and one night some maniac threw seven sticks of dynamite among the tents, but they didn't go off. We called a mass meeting to decide what we were going to do. I was speaking when we were invaded by a mob— including the law—wielding guns and ax handles. People were so frightened they went straight out the windows. I kept on talking, and one of the men asked me if I was going "peaceably" or would they have to take me, and I said I wasn't going. So they put this other fellow and me in a car and drove us to a deserted spot in the woods, where one of them started fixing a noose over a tree limb. I told them I was from Tennessee, and if they hung me and got caught, they'd be tried in a federal court. They talked it over and decided they'd let us go if we'd leave Arkansas and never return, but we wouldn't promise. Finally, they took us back to the Mississippi River bridge and told us they'd kill us if we ever came back.

H. L. Mitchell was in Memphis while all this was going on, and when he got word that I had been taken away by the mob, he was sure I had been lynched. He wired Norman Thomas, who was speaking at a dinner in New York, and the telegram was read at the dinner. By the time I got home to Nashville, Alice had already received several calls expressing sympathy. Needless to say, she was surprised to see me.

Kester's involvement with the tenant farmers extended over the better part of four years. Once again he found himself contending with the communists, for they tried to gain control of the union—and ultimately succeeded:

The United Canning and Packing Workers of America— called *U-cap-a-wa*, phonetically—had a communist secretary, one Donald Henderson, a former teacher at Columbia University, and the union under him made an all-out effort to take over our union in about 1939. Our people were very unsophisticated; a few of them saw what we were doing as an attempt to revive populism, but most of them had very simple and straightforward concerns and objectives—they wanted a written contract, a measure of security on the plantation, justice in the courts, the right to have a garden, an education for their children. Racial unity was also one of the goals, and for many of the people it had become not only a good idea strategically but also the democratic and Christian thing to do—they believed in it. But money and prestige naturally appealed to some of our people, and Ucapawa had that to offer. They wanted our little group to affiliate. I did all I could to discourage it, giving several reasons why we shouldn't be swallowed up by the big union, but the people voted to join. Mitchell agreed with me, but his voice and mine lost out to the big international organization, and within a year, our predictions had come true. The tenant farmers then changed their minds and withdrew, but the damage was done, and our union didn't survive. I think it was one of the most important egalitarian movements in American history, but it came to nothing because of communism.

In all the causes Buck Kester joined, religious considerations played a central part. He was, after all, a minister, having reached that calling only after a series of disappointments and setbacks that are themselves an indication of his determination to gain the sanction of the organized church. Yet he never was a pastor; he was a maverick, a man who found his parish in the mines and sharecropper shacks of the South. Far from using his religion as a cloak to hide other ambitions, he wore his faith openly, as something inseparable from the rest of human concerns, and it was that stance that brought him together with the remnant of Southern churchmen who formed a new religious fellowship in the middle of the 1930s.

They met at Monteagle, Tennessee, and formed the Committee of Younger Churchmen in the South. They were admirers—many of them former students—of Reinhold Niebuhr, and Niebuhr's Committee on Economic and Racial Justice, whose only employee was Kester, nourished the creation and development of the new group. Kester was made secretary, and about a year later the name of the organization was changed to the Fellowship of Southern Churchmen. It was, first and last, a religious fellowship, steeped in commitment to New Testament Christianity and the teachings of Christ. Luke 4:18 was the creed: ". . . to preach the gospel to the poor, to heal the broken-hearted, to preach deliverance to the captive, and recovery of sight to the blind, to set at liberty them that are bruised, to preach the acceptable year of the Lord." It was an inclusive fellowship, with no bars of race, sex, or economics. Kester recalls: "This, to me, was really the only thing I ever wanted to do. I had lost faith in the promises of politics, unionism, and the organized church. The kind of healing the region and the nation needed wouldn't come through politics or economic organization—basically, there had to be an ethical orientation, a moral confrontation, based on the teachings of Jesus and the principles of democracy."

Through the late 1930s and into the 1940s, the Fellowship functioned as a loose confederation of men and women who "were close to the problems of the people." They identified with farmers, with laborers, with the unemployed; they spoke in churches and schools and meeting halls and in the outdoors. They preached brotherhood, and practiced it, all over the South. In addition to Kester, who served as secretary during those years, the Fellowship included Gene Smathers, T. B. "Scotty" Cowan, James Weldon Johnson, Walter Sikes, James Dombroski, Gene Cox, and Sam Franklin, to name only a few. In 1941, Kester became the first full-time executive secretary of the Fellowship, and he stayed in that job until 1944. Earlier, in 1939, he had built the house at High Top Colony and moved there from Nashville with Alice and Nancy.

The Fellowship never even came close to becoming a disciplined, monolithic organization. Its members were like-minded but not single-minded; they were individuals who sought the comfort and support of companions of the same general philosophy, but they remained individuals, and their individuality tended to make waves. In a brief history of the Fellowship written by David Burgess, one of their number, this paragraph appears:

> As the members of the Fellowship matured important differences developed amongst them. Some thought Kester and Cowan had gone off on what they called a "Jesus Jag" and indicated their disgust with a movement that approached every problem from a religious perspective. Some of these found their way into secular movements of varying degrees of social importance. A few members were captivated by the glowing promises of communism but the leaders of the Fellowship had made up their minds about the validity of their Christian and democratic faith, and once having done so, nothing could budge them even to the point of refusing membership to close personal friends who were known communists or fellow-travelers. Thus, long before the nation had aroused itself to the diabolical intentions of world communism, the members of the Fellowship had recognized the complete incompatibility of the basic tenets of communism with the principles of both democracy and Christianity. When the "united front" was the liberal's religion, the Fellowship leaders stood firm against it and were labeled "fascists" for doing so.

The depth of personal disagreement and the intensity of anti-communist feeling are both illuminated by that paragraph. Kester's recollection of this period is vivid:

> The experience of some of the members was so different from mine and Cowan's and a few others' that they just couldn't understand how anybody could have the attitude we

did. We were trying to call attention to the implications of the Christian faith for all humanity. We had no political plank—it was just love, *agape*. Men will tell you today that it won't work, it's impractical, and that's all I've ever heard in my life, but I know it *will* work, and it *does* work, and people respond to it—trying to equate the word made flesh with everything in your home, with your neighbors, everybody with whom you come in contact. Nothing made any difference to us but human need, that was the measure, and you went because people were in need, it didn't matter who they were, or where or how they lived.

Buck resigned his job with the Fellowship in 1944 to become principal of the Penn School, a Quaker-supported private school for Negroes on St. Helena Island, off Beaufort, South Carolina. It may have been the internal friction in the Fellowship that made him decide to go, it may have been the opportunity he saw at the school, it may have been something else. Whatever the case, he went with Alice and Nancy, left the house on the mountain and the job and the commitments to half a dozen similar causes which he managed to carry at the same time, and for four years he ran the Penn School:

> It was overrated as an educational institution, over-idealized not only by those who were perhaps too close to see its weaknesses, but by outside observers as well. We were stunned. There was no money, the accreditation was in jeopardy, it was just coasting. Alice took over as the supervisor of instruction, and after some hard effort we got some competent educators to come in and make a candid evaluation, and we came up with a plan to revitalize the place. The trustees adopted it, and once the new program was well underway, we left.

In 1948 he and Alice went back to the house on the mountain. Nancy was away at school by then, and Alice was in poor health, as she had been much of the time for several years. The house was their anchor, the one place they truly felt at home, and they went intending to stay. But a year later, the Congregational Church asked him to come to New York and direct a displaced persons bureau set up to find homes and jobs in this country for European refugees of the war. Working as a team, as they had done for twenty years, Buck and Alice revamped the slipshod program and found work and homes for nearly 1,500 families in a year's time. Then they went back to North Carolina, and Kester spent eighteen months as director of the Campbell Folk School at Brasstown. His ideas for restructuring that sleepy little institution were too radical for the directors, so he left.

During the years he was away, the Fellowship of Southern Churchmen continued to grow under the leadership of Nelle Morton at the University of North Carolina, and later under Charles Jones, a Presbyterian minister in Chapel Hill. A gift of 383 acres of land near Swannanoa provided the Fellowship with a permanent home, and in 1952 Buck returned to the Fellowship as executive director and took on the job of developing the land, building cabins and meeting facilities, and running work camps and retreats. He was also busy on the speaker's circuit, and Alice's health had not improved, but for five more years he kept at it in spite of a steady increase of job and family responsibilities. During this period the U.S. Supreme Court outlawed school segregation, the civil-rights movement began in earnest, and the Fellowship found itself in trouble:

> We had a hard time getting money. The foundations were scared of us—they thought we were too radical. I guess when segregation was almost completely unchallenged we were too small to be considered either a threat to the status quo or a promise of real change. But after the court changed the legal picture, we were seen to be several steps ahead of the idea of "all deliberate speed."
> It appeared for awhile after the 1954 decision that the South was going to face up to its responsibilities. I was in Black Mountain at that time, and my view was that people would go along. People I knew, laboring people, didn't dis-

sent—one garage foreman told me, "You can't read your
Bible and come out any other way"—and there were many
others like him, and I had great hopes. Kids were already adjusting. I felt we were about to turn the corner. And then the
reaction set in. Politicians were responsible for a lot of it, but
the great failure, in my view, was the church. All too often,
church leaders were worse than passive—they actually led the
opposition. I remember one conference of the Methodist
Church in Birmingham at which some of its outstanding members went out of their way to voice defiance of the court decision. If even a significant minority in the churches had taken
a stand, it could have been different.

In 1956, Buck and Alice made a four-month trip across
the South. In a newsletter to members of the Fellowship
written after that journey, Kester made it clear that the
"democratic-Christian minority" working for racial justice
was a small remnant forced underground by the violent
temper of the times. He praised the spirit and courage of
that remnant—in particular the families of Gene Cox and
David Minter at Providence Farm, a cooperative farm in
Holmes County, Mississippi—and clung to the hope that the
organized church would direct its energies toward reconciliation, but it was obvious from the tone of his letter that the
tide was running swiftly in the opposite direction. The
"fundamental fact," he wrote, is "that the feudal character of
our society has yielded stubbornly, hesitatingly and slowly,
when at all, to the ideas of Jesus, Jefferson, and Einstein."

The story of Providence Farm, of Koinonia Farm in Georgia, and of other cooperatives around the South, and of the
people who created and nurtured these interracial communities, is an inspiring story that needs to be fully told. Like the
Fellowship of Southern Churchmen—to which many members of the farm communities belonged—they were the remnant, the "democratic-Christian minority."

In 1957, the Fellowship called an integrated conference
of churchmen, to meet in Nashville for three days of discus-

sion of racial tensions. The National Council of Churches was asked to help support and sponsor the conference, but the council wouldn't touch it, though Will Campbell, who was their man in the South, volunteered the use of his office and the Tennessee Council of Churches cooperated, as did Scarritt College and some divinity school professors at Vanderbilt University.

For the time and place, it was a significant event. Three hundred churchmen from all over the South came—4,500 had been invited—and they heard a succession of speakers tell them what first the Lord and then the law required of them: justice for all men. One of the speakers was a Baptist minister from Montgomery named Martin Luther King Jr. "We have the responsibility of freeing our white brothers from the quibblings of unreasonable fears," he said. "Segregation scars the soul of the segregator and the segregated. The churches can make brotherhood a reality. We are grappling with the most serious issue of our society. We must not become bitter. We must not be tempted to violence. We have the glorious opportunity to inject love into the stream of our nation's life." That became the theme of the civil-rights movement, and King became its principal messenger.

The Nashville conference was a kind of culminating act of the Fellowship. It was all the more significant because the line separating the advocates of racial equality from the forces of white supremacy had already been deeply drawn, and the irony of the meeting was that its message of reconciliation came after the reality of alienation had been made plain across the South.

The Fellowship, lacking funds, couldn't afford a full-time secretary any longer, and in the fall after the Nashville conference Kester accepted a job as director of student life at Eureka College, a small church college in Illinois—best known now as Ronald Reagan's alma mater. The Fellowship was left in the hands of a committee, which tried with only limited success to hold the remnant together. Kester

stayed three years at Eureka, ending up as a history professor and dean of students. He had gone in anticipation of a
lighter work load, but it was, if anything, heavier. In 1960
he returned to North Carolina to manage Christmount Assembly, a project of the Christian Church (Disciples of
Christ), the same denomination that supports Eureka College. He also taught part-time at nearby Montreat-Anderson
College, and in 1965 he finally joined the college full-time
as a professor in the social sciences. Later, he became dean
of students.

The philosophy and character of Howard Kester defy conventional stereotyping. Call him Southerner, socialist, Christian, radical, democrat, anti-communist—all of these are
accurate, but each is insufficient to describe the man or to explain his commitment to an ideal that is both too old and
too new to be popular. He built his philosophy around the
example of Jesus, and repeatedly he was told that he was
too radical, too far ahead of his time.

Kester doesn't seem very radical any more. The times have
changed—or have they? A few months after I visited him,
the Southern Student Organizing Committee, an organization of student radicals on Southern campuses, held a meeting in Mississippi to decide its future, including its relationship to the Students for a Democratic Society. Once again,
the Yankees won the war: SDS brought in several carloads
of "voters" for the exercise in "participatory democracy,"
and proceeded to capture SSOC by voting it out of existence.
It was a clear victory of ideology, doctrine, and abstract
theory over the gut feelings of humanism and idealism. If
the SSOC kids had counseled with Buck Kester before it
happened they could have gotten a first hand account of an
earlier version of the same drama thirty years ago, when
Ucapawa took over the Southern Tenant Farmers' Union.

It was near dark when I left Buck and Alice at High Top
Colony, and a misty drizzle was falling. On the front porch,
I asked him one more question: Could it be, as some people

maintain, that the South might yet prove to be the most fertile ground for racial equality in this country? "I've long said it," he answered, "and so have many Negroes. The only white man who comes close to understanding what racial justice really means is the Southerner. Once a white Southerner has made up his mind on this, you can bank on him, because he not only knows it intellectually—he feels it in his soul." Buck Kester is a Southern white man who made up his mind fifty years ago.

Fannie Lou Hamer

The best-known citizen of Sunflower County, Mississippi, is the Honorable James O. Eastland, sixty-six years old, twenty-nine years a member of the United States Senate and chairman of that august body's powerful Judiciary Committee for nigh onto a generation. He is a Democrat, a white supremacist, and a wealthy plantation owner. His income in recent years has been supplemented by the U.S. Department of Agriculture, which has paid him more than $100,000 annually for not planting cotton.

The second best-known citizen of Sunflower County is Mrs. Fannie Lou Hamer, fifty-three years old, seven years a registered voter, a founder and vice-chairman of the Mississippi Freedom Democratic Party. By almost any yardstick, she measures poor; she is not "gainfully employed," as the economists say, and in all her lifetime she probably will never earn as much money as the Department of Agriculture paid to Senator Eastland last year alone. Mrs. Hamer's income is derived from food stamps, faithful friends, and people who pay to hear her speak—people trying to learn vicariously what it is like to be black and female and poor and out of patience in Mississippi.

Senator Eastland and Mrs. Hamer have never met, even

though his plantation home in Sunflower County is only five miles or so from her tiny house. It would be safe to say that they know each other by reputation, however, and the chances are good that they will be hearing more from each other as time goes on. Mrs. Hamer thinks so, anyway. "He ain't heard nothin' yet," she says.

Another Mississippian, William Faulkner, must have had people like Fannie Lou Hamer in mind when he wrote "The Bear." In that story, he has one of his characters say that cotton shackled black people after the Civil War as completely as leg irons had bound their forebears: ". . . threads frail as truth and impalpable as equators yet cable-strong to bind for life them who made the cotton to the land their sweat fell on." And Faulkner responds, through another of his characters: "Yes. Binding them for awhile yet, a little while yet. Through and beyond that life and maybe through and beyond the life of that life's sons and maybe even through and beyond that of the sons of those sons. But not always, because they will endure."

It was, I believe, Faulkner's way of affirming the humanity of black people: "They will endure." Mrs. Hamer, he no doubt would say, is a credit to her race—the human race. Of that larger species, Faulkner said this in his acceptance speech when he was awarded the Nobel Prize in 1950: "I believe that man will not merely endure: he will prevail. He is immortal, not because he alone among creatures has an inexhaustible voice, but because he has a soul, a spirit capable of compassion and sacrifice and endurance."

He was not talking just about white men or black men, but about all men, and had he known Mrs. Hamer he would have seen her as living proof of his affirmation. She has endured savage violence at the hands of white men, endured subjugation, dispossession, and terror, and she is still there, using Adam Clayton Powell's benediction: "Keep the faith, baby." Mr. Faulkner and Mrs. Hamer, two Mississippians, would have understood each other very well.

In 1963—the twenty-second year of James Eastland's ten-
ure in the Senate, and the year after William Faulkner
died—Mrs. Hamer became a registered voter in Sunflower
County. The county's population was about 45,000 at that
time, and two-thirds of them were black, yet she was one of
the first to gain the right to vote. In the four months it had
taken her to win that right, she and her husband had lost
their jobs and their home, their lives had been threatened,
and they were faced with the choice of fleeing or fighting
back. They chose to fight. In the process, she became a re-
cruit in the ranks of the civil-rights movement.

Now the Movement has dissipated, and the whirr of television cameras is seldom heard in the Mississippi Delta. But
what was started there in the early 1960's didn't stop when
the Movement moved on; in big ways and small, black citizens who have caught a vision of freedom still reach for it.

At ten o'clock on a still and steamy August morning, Mrs.
Hamer sat under the leafy spread of a pecan tree in her front
yard in Ruleville, sipping ice water from a fruit jar and holding a plate of fried fish and scrambled eggs on one knee. She
had been up late the night before, at a mass meeting to promote the Freedom Farms Cooperative, an economic development enterprise of and for the poor people of Sunflower
County. Mrs. Hamer is its principal organizer, fund-raiser
and spokesman.

Her husband, a big man who conserves his words, came
out from the front porch of their three-room, unpainted
house, and their two granddaughters (the children of their
oldest of two daughters, who died in 1967) were playing in
the shade of the tree. As we talked and the morning wore
on, other people came and went, some driving, others walking—neighbors, friends, fellow workers in the co-op—and
the conversations turned repeatedly to Freedom Farms and
the meeting of the night before. Inside the house, the phone
rang every few minutes.

After a while we drove out to the first and primary project of the co-op, a 44-acre mini-farm, part of it planted in cotton and beans, the rest set aside for a "pig bank" to produce food and income for the project's member families. The little farm, on a gravel road that cuts through the flat cotton fields, is nineteen miles from Ruleville.

A mile or so from their ramshackle house, the Hamers had moved a larger and more durable house onto a lot they had acquired, and workmen were expanding it and adding a brick veneer. Much of the money for that project was raised by the editors of *Katallagete,* the journal of the Nashville-based Committee of Southern Churchmen. An appeal they sent to their subscribers brought in about $6,000, including $41.95 from seventeen inmates of the Wisconsin State Prison.

Back at the house, Mrs. Hamer answered a couple of phone calls and then took the receiver off the hook, and we settled on the front porch to talk, away from the now-larger group of people on the benches and chairs under the pecan tree.

"I went to my first mass meetin' in that little church right over there," she said, pointing to a concrete block structure down the street.

> It was in 1962. James Bevel was there from SCLC, and James Forman from SNCC, and one or two others, and they told us it was our constitutional right to register and vote. I had never even seen the Constitution of the United States, or of Mississippi, but I signed up with the group that was gonna try to register.
>
> It wasn't because black people in Mississippi was satisfied that we hadn't tried before that—it was just that we knew what would happen. We had learned how to survive, how to laugh at trouble. But it wasn't easy, let me tell you.
>
> I was born fifty-three years ago in Montgomery County, Mississippi, last of twenty children. We moved to Sunflower when I was two, and lived about four miles east of here, on a plantation. We were sharecroppers, and we never had enough to eat.

My mother would go around to the plantations and get them to let us scrap the fields, and sometimes we'd walk twenty miles a day just to get a bale of scrappin' cotton—you know, what's left when the field has been picked over. I started pickin' when I was six. The man told me if I'd pick thirty pounds I could come to his commissary store and get cracker jacks and candy, and I'd never had all that, so I picked the thirty pounds, and then the next week it was sixty, and by the time I was thirteen I could pick as much as a man.

I couldn't understand what was happening. We didn't have shoes, so we'd wrap our feet in rags, and it was never warm enough, and I used to ask my mother how come everybody wasn't white, because they were the ones who had plenty of food and clothes, and they had the big houses, and yet they didn't have to work hard or do much of anything. And my mother said, "There's nothin' wrong with you bein' black, child. God made you black. Respect yourself." She bought me a black doll, the only one I ever had seen.

My mother used to come in from the fields too tired to walk, but after we ate she'd sit down with a bundle and patch clothes 'til late. She'd do anything to get us to school and to church. She was very tired, she had been worked nearly to death, but she had to keep movin' for her family to survive. And my daddy, he finally got to where he had enough to buy three mules and two cows, but a man who lived near us put Paris green in their water and killed them. My folks was too old to make a comeback. I watched them suffer, and I got angry. I'd look at my mother and say to myself, "If I ever live to get grown, I'll never see you in patched clothes or workin' that hard." I got married in 1944, and my mother lived with us for ten years after that—my father had died in 1939—and I worked to where I couldn't sleep at night, but I never let her wear a patched dress.

As a child, Fannie Lou went to the Baptist Church— "Stranger's Home, it was called, and that's just what it was" —and she was baptized in the Quiver River when she was twelve. That was also the year she went to school for the last time. The school term lasted only four or five months,

John Egerton

Al Clayton

James McBride Dabbs

John Lewis

Howard (Buck) Kester

Lucius H. Pitts

U. W. Clemon

Sarah Patton Boyle

John Howard Griffin

Billie and De De Pierce

and after six years of that she had learned to read and write but little else.

"From early childhood, our folks taught us to do unto others, and not to hate," she recalls. "It might not matter what you do to me, but it makes a whole lot of difference for my insides what I do to you. If I hate you, then we're just two miserable people. Hate is something destructive. I grew up believin' in God, but I knew things was bad wrong, and I used to think, 'Let me have a chance, and whatever this is that's wrong in Mississippi, I'm gonna do somethin' about it.' And that's the way I was feelin' the night those young fellows came in here to the church and told us about registerin' to vote."

They went in to the county seat at Indianola, eighteen of them riding in an old school bus one of the men owned, and presented themselves at the clerk's office. He sent them out, telling them to come back two at a time to take the literacy test and to read, copy, and interpret a section of the Mississippi Constitution. It took the entire afternoon for all of them to finish, and then, without being told whether or not they had passed the test, they started home:

> The police stopped us outside the city limits and took us back to Indianola. The driver was arrested—they said he was drivin' the wrong color bus—and he was fined $100. We begged and pleaded with them to let us go, and finally they cut the fine to $30. We had enough money among us to pay that, so we did, and then we came on home.
>
> When I got to the house, my daughter met me. She said the plantation owner—his name is W. D. Marlow III—was very mad because we had gone to register. He told her if I didn't withdraw my registration, he'd put me off the place. And you know, that was what really did it for me. I just thought to myself, "What does he really care about us?" I had been workin' there for eighteen years. I had baked cakes and sent them overseas to him during the war, I had nursed his family, cleaned his house, stayed with his kids. I had

handled his time book and his payroll. Yet he wanted me out. I made up my mind I was grown, and I was tired. I wouldn't go back. In a little while he came to the house, ravin' mad, tellin' me I'd have to withdraw, and I said to him, "Mr. D, I didn't go to register for you—I went for me." I had no choice. That night, I left.

She went into Ruleville to stay with a friend, leaving her husband and two daughters behind, and the next week her husband drove her to the home of a niece in a neighboring county. Soon after, the home where she had stayed in Ruleville was fired into, and there were other instances of retaliation against the eighteen who had tried to register—even though, as it turned out, all of them had been refused. In Oxford, eighty-five miles away, James Meredith had entered the University of Mississippi. It was a time of hope and a time of terror for Mississippi Negroes.

After three months, Mrs. Hamer returned to Ruleville:

Marlow had refused to pay my daughters for working, and then he fired my husband and took our car, so they came in here too, and we rented this house from a black woman, and we've been here ever since. That same month—December 1962—I went back to the court house to take the literacy test again. I told the clerk, "You'll see me every thirty days 'til I register. You can't have me fired any more." They refused me again, but the next month, on the third trip, I was registered. Some people had to take that test twenty-six times, but they kept goin' back.

From then on, every day brought trouble. Mrs. Hamer became an active worker for SNCC, mostly doing voter registration and literacy training jobs, and she was a prime target of white terrorists. Her husband and one of her daughters were arrested, she was harassed by such things as a $9,000 water bill (her house didn't even have running water), their church had to be shut down because the fire insurance was canceled and the members were intimidated. On one occasion, two policemen with drawn guns and flashlights walked into the Hamers' bedroom before daylight, on the pretense of making a search—without a warrant. "There was always something," Mrs. Hamer says,

and on top of all the harassment we didn't have work. People brought us food, and we were finally able to get commodities from the welfare office—the man literally threw it at us. Various people and programs met our everyday bills. And SNCC helped a lot—they were the only civil-rights organization that was really interested in doin' somethin' about conditions in the Delta. They started the grass roots movement in Mississippi—people like Bob Moses, Jim Forman, John Lewis. I tried to help them, and the other groups too—SCLC, CORE, the NAACP—and when COFO [the Council of Federated Organizations] was formed, I was a part of it.

She was also part of a group of workers who went to South Carolina for a voter registration workshop and training program in June of 1963, and when they got back to Mississippi, the violence Mrs. Hamer had lived in the shadow of since her first attempt to register finally caught her.

They arrived at the bus station in Winona, sixty miles from Ruleville, on a Sunday morning, and some members of the group got off the bus to go into the café and to the rest room. The local chief of police and a state highway patrolman, who were sitting in the café, told them to get out. They did, and when Annelle Ponder, an SCLC worker and one of the group, stopped outside to write down the license number of the patrol car, the two officers rushed out and arrested them.

Mrs. Hamer, who had stayed on the bus, got off and called to Miss Ponder. The police chief, seeing her, yelled to another officer to "get that one there, bring her on down in the other car!" Altogether, six persons—all but one of them women—were taken to the county jail. Mrs. Hamer recalls:

These two men put me in the car, and while I was gettin' in, one of them kicked me. They would ask me questions and cuss me, and before I could answer they'd tell me to shut up.

When we got to the jail they started beatin' the man—his name was James West—and they put us in cells, two to a cell, and I could hear all this hollerin' and goin' on. This one girl passed by us, bleedin' somethin' awful. Then they took Miss Ponder. I could hear these awful sounds and licks and screams, hear her body hit the concrete, and this man was yellin', "Can't you say yes sir, you nigger bitch?" But she never would say yes sir to 'em, and finally they passed my cell with her, and her mouth was all swollen and her clothes were torn to the waist and her eye looked like blood, it was *horrible*. And I knew I had it comin'.

Then they came to me, three white men. This highway patrolman—the name on his badge was John L. Bassinger, I'll never forget it—he asked me where I was from, and when I told him he said, "I'm gonna check and see," and he came back in a few minutes and I knew he had found out all about me 'cause he said, "You nigger bitch, we gonna make you wish you was dead."

They carried me out of the cell into a room with two Negro prisoners, and told me to lie down on my face on this cot that was in there. The patrolman gave one of the prisoners a long leather blackjack with lead or something in it, and he told him to beat me with it. That poor man had already been beat up, and they told him, "If you don't do it, you black son of a bitch, you know what we'll do to you." So he beat me 'til he give out, exhausted. I was tryin' to hold my hands behind me, and my hands turned *blue* and hard as a bone— I couldn't bend 'em. So then they ordered the other prisoner to beat me, and I started kickin' and I couldn't stop screamin' —I was nearly out of my mind. In all this my dress had worked up, and I tried to pull it down, and one of them white men—there was five of them in there—he took and pulled it up to my head. They just kept on beatin' me and tellin' me I'd wish I was dead. There ain't nothin' like the kind of misery I was goin' through. When they finally quit, they told me to go back to my cell, but I couldn't get up, I couldn't bend my knees.

They stayed in jail for three days, charged with "disorderly conduct and resisting arrest." Lawrence Guyot, who later became chairman of the Mississippi Freedom Democratic Party, was brought into the same jail during that time, and he too was beaten. When James Bevel and Andrew Young of SCLC finally managed to get them out of jail, they had received no medical attention. "My body was as hard as this chair I'm sittin' in," Mrs. Hamer said. "They took us to Greenwood to see a doctor, and then to Atlanta. I wouldn't let my husband see me for a month, I was in such bad shape. Every day of my life I pay with the misery of that beatin'. And it was while we was in that jail that Medgar Evers was killed, and one night they offered to let us go, just so they could kill us and say we was tryin' to escape. I told 'em they'd have to kill me in my cell."

The next year, Mrs. Hamer told that tale of horror in front of television cameras at the Democratic National Convention, when the Freedom Democrats made their dramatic but unsuccessful attempt to challenge the seating of the regular state delegation. She also told it to the FBI, and to the Justice Department, and the white lawmen who had beaten them were later brought to trial in federal court at Oxford. An all-white jury found them innocent.

Recalling that, Mrs. Hamer said: "I just wonder how many more times is America gonna turn its head and pretend nothin' is happenin'. I used to think the Justice Department was just what it said—justice. I asked one of those men, 'Have y'all got a Justice Department or a *In*justice Department?' That's the way I feel now. They didn't investigate what *happened* to us—they investigated *us*. So I tell people I don't want no *equal* rights any more. I'm fightin' for *human* rights. I don't want to become equal to men like them that beat us. I don't want to become the kind of person that would kill you because of your color."

The year 1964 produced some of the civil-rights movement's greatest victories, as well as some of its costliest losses. It was the year Congress passed its most comprehensive civil-rights bill, Lyndon Johnson defeated Barry Goldwater, and Martin Luther King won the Nobel Prize.

It was also the year that three civil-rights workers were murdered in Philadelphia, Mississippi; Lemuel Penn, a black educator from Washington, was gunned down on a Georgia highway; and racial rioting broke out in Harlem, Rochester, and North Philadelphia—auguries of Watts, Newark, and Detroit. Many people would be heard to say later that the Civil Rights Act solved nothing, that LBJ's victory changed nothing, that Dr. King's honor proved nothing, and as far as many black people were concerned, those assessments were very nearly accurate. Threats and harassment continued to dog the Hamers as if nothing had happened. The Freedom Democratic Party was organized to challenge the Mississippi "regulars," who openly professed their disloyalty to the national party, yet all Mrs. Hamer and her companions could come away with was a compromise that would have given them token representation in the Mississippi delegation. The Freedom Democrats rejected that out of hand, and went back home to Mississippi. They tried unsuccessfully to get their candidates' names on the ballot for the congressional elections that fall, and then they made up their own ballots and had their own election. In the state's Second Congressional District, Mrs. Hamer drew over 33,000 votes in the Freedom Party's balloting, and her opponent, incumbent Representative Jamie Whitten, got only 49. Whitten, of course, won the regular election without serious opposition.

The Freedom Democrats went to Washington the following January to challenge the seating of the five "regular" Mississippi representatives, and, though they didn't succeed, they did get an eight-month investigation that ended on September 17, 1965, when Mrs. Hamer and other members of the Freedom Democratic Party went onto the floor of the House of Representatives for the climax of their challenge. "The challenge was dismissed," she remembers, "and I saw another part of democracy go down the drain. Later on they unseated Adam Clayton Powell, but only censured Thomas Dodd—and there's Eastland, he's been in there thirty years, but 70 per cent of his people can't vote. So this ain't just Mississippi's problem. It's America's problem."

While she was talking, a white farmer drove up in front of her house with a load of fresh vegetables on his pickup truck, and a few of Mrs. Hamer's neighbors went out to make their purchases. "You see that man?" she said. "He's a pretty good man, but he's scared. Says he's for us but he can't speak out. You know what I tell him? I say, 'We're fightin' for *your* freedom, too, 'cause you're not even free enough to say how you feel about things.' He knows I'm right, too."

The Freedom Democrats formed a coalition with a "Loyalist" faction of the regular party and managed to unseat the "Regulars" at the 1968 convention in Chicago. But the coalition didn't last; the Freedom Democrats are now an independent political action group, and Mrs. Hamer, who was one of the Chicago delegates, isn't very hopeful about the future: "We're still powerless, and the Loyalists haven't done nothin'. I'm the kind of person who believes that somewhere there's *got* to be *somebody* that's fit for something, but if there ain't, then we're gonna have to do what we got to do—form a third party. It's unbelievable what a person will do in politics."

What seems more likely than the formation of a third party is the desertion of the Democratic Party by most whites. Segregation is till the dominant style in Mississippi —the vast majority of school children were in segregated schools until this year, only one member of the legislature is black, and almost all local officials such as mayors and sheriffs are white. Charles Evers, the mayor of Fayette, is the most notable exception to the pattern. He and Aaron Henry, the state NAACP president, are leaders in the Loyalist wing of the Democratic Party. It is easier to imagine the Loyalists and the Freedom Democrats patching up their differences than it is to picture a truly integrated, statewide political party.

In eight years of involvement in the Mississippi racial

struggle, Mrs. Hamer has had plenty of cause for discourage-
ment, but she hasn't given up. She remains active in her
church, "tellin' the preachers they can't stay on that stuff
they're preachin' and keep from doin' anything." The
church, she says, "hasn't done much, and they're gonna have
to get goin' or there won't be anybody in it." She was one
of the original signers of the Black Manifesto, which James
Forman and others presented to the white churches of America in demanding reparations for blacks.

> I didn't know what the manifesto was, but when Jim For-
> man called and asked me to endorse it, I said if it was for
> humanity, then I was for it. A lot of people got upset about
> me signin' that, but I didn't back down. That thing shook a
> lot of people up. I'm not for interruptin' any church services,
> but black preachers have been used in the past to keep us
> in our place, and that's all over now.
>
> I don't believe in separatism—a house divided against it-
> self cannot stand, and neither can a nation. This country
> produces separatists. America is sick, and man is on the crit-
> ical list.

She quoted from Ephesians about struggling against "prin-
cipalities" and "powers" and "spiritual wickedness in high
places," and from St. Luke—"he has anointed me to preach
the gospel to the poor"—and from Acts: "God has made
of one blood all nations of men. . . ." Mrs. Hamer added:
"Christianity is bein' concerned about your fellow man, not
buildin' a million-dollar church while people are starvin'
right around the corner. Christ was a revolutionary person,
out there where it was happenin'. That's what God is all
about, and that's where I get my strength."

That strength has become something to be reckoned with
in Sunflower County. Mrs. Hamer spends all of her time on
organization of political and economic black power there,
and on raising funds from outside the state to keep the
movement going. More than 7,000 Negroes in the county
are now registered to vote, and as that number has climbed,
white terrorism has diminished. The Freedom Farms Co-

operative, as small as it is, still presents a potential challenge
to white economic domination, and a growing number of
Black Belt counties across the South are following a similar
pattern.

For two years I went around the country beggin' money to
buy food stamps. I got $20,000, but folks still needed food. I
saw that wasn't gonna work—we had to do somethin' for ourselves. So we decided to try to grow vegetables and peanuts
and raise some of our own meat. The National Council of
Negro Women sent a delegation down here, and then they
gave us some pigs. Fifty families got one sow each, and we
got five boars, and that was the start of our pig bank. Then
this black farmer offered us that land out there, and I called
this friend of mine at the Harvard Law School—Lester Solo-
mon is his name—and he ran a story in the Harvard paper,
and that brought in some money, and we got some from an
organization in Atlanta that helps these co-op programs, and
some people in Madison, Wisconsin, gave some. That was
enough to buy the 44 acres, and then Harry Belafonte helped
us, too. Now we've got the co-op goin', and last night we had
a full house for our first mass meetin'. The idea is to feed
poor people—black and white—and nothin' is gonna be sold
until we take care of that need first. We're tryin' to get 3,000
members—that's our first goal—with each member payin' $3
a year. We also are buyin' some houses where we can, and
we've got a location now where we hope to build a co-op
center, and we think maybe some of the other black landowners will come in with us. This thing is for whoever needs
it—race hasn't got anything to do with it. A few whites have
said they'll support us, and one man gave me a donation. He
said he can see for the first time what I'm doin'—he finally
understands. Out of the baddest of people there's some good
quality there, and out of the best there's some bad. We have
to look for the best.

For all its ambitions, the Freedom Farms Cooperative and
the other economic and political stirrings of Sunflower
County's black citizens are a long way from freedom. They
are a majority in a political jurisdiction where the majority

does not rule. Many blacks have left the rural South in search of the Promised Land. Mrs. Hamer says she's not leaving:

> Some people say there's more possibility for human rights in the South than in the North. That may not be so, but I'll take a chance on it first. There's one thing about folks in the South: if they're dirt, they don't mind lettin' you know it. Some of them in the North, they're not a bit different, but they got that smile on 'em, and I don't like a hypocrite. Not that I like the racism, but I'd rather any day for a man to be honest and tell me he hates me, than for him *not* to be honest and then shoot me when I turn around.
>
> I never thought of leavin' the South. I love it. I was born here. I watched my folks take a double-blade ax and chop down trees like that pecan there. A lot of this land the white folks is usin' now, I watched my parents clean it up. We're not tryin' to take this land away from them, but we got a right to stay here. That's what I told the principal when I put my girl in school. He accused her of stealin', and I said she didn't do it. He said, "I hate a liar and a thief," and I told him, "Then you don't hate *my* people, you hate *yours.* If your people hadn't stole from my people, we'd own this country."
>
> People who tell me to go back to Africa, I got an answer for them. I say when all the Italians go back to Italy, and all the Germans go back to Germany, and all the Frenchmen go back to France, and all the Chinese go back to China, and when they give the Indians their land back and they get on the Mayflower and go back to where they came from, then I'll go home too.
>
> So I ain't givin' up. I'm stayin' right here in the South, in Mississippi. We got to treat each other right, 'cause we're in this thing together, and if the white people survive, we're gonna survive too.

Fannie Lou Hamer spoke the fundamental truth about the black people of Mississippi: They ain't givin' up. William Faulkner said it too: They will endure.

Lucius H. Pitts
and U. W. Clemon

Birmingham, 1963. Steel and smoke and white supremacy. George Wallace and Al Lingo, Bull Connor and Jamie Moore, Arthur Hanes and Albert Boutwell. Police dogs and fire hoses and cattle prods. Tear gas and armored cars and fire bombs. Thousands of arrests. Martin Luther King and Ralph David Abernathy and Fred Shuttlesworth and Arthur Shores and A. G. Gaston and Orzelle Billingsley and Andrew Young and James Bevel and Dick Gregory and scores of others, lesser known but no less courageous. Wallace saying he would "not be a party to any . . . meeting to compromise on issues of segregation," and white terrorists taking their cue from that defiant attitude to establish their own deadly brand of "law and order." King writing his "Letter From Birmingham City Jail," a document which makes a good companion piece to the letter Paul wrote to the Ephesians when he was "a prisoner for the Lord," nineteen centuries ago. President John F. Kennedy, Attorney General Robert F. Kennedy, mediators, negotiators, federal troops, federalized national guardsmen. An explosion in the Sixteenth Street Baptist Church, killing four little girls. Riots, more bombings, more killing of Negroes by whites. Charles Morgan, a white lawyer, saying to the Young Men's Business Club of

Birmingham: "And who is really guilty? Each of us . . . each citizen who has ever said 'they ought to kill that nigger' . . . every person in this community who has in any way contributed during the past several months to the popularity of hatred. . . ." A man in the audience rising after the speech to suggest that a Negro be admitted to the club, and the motion dying for want of a second. Bombingham, 1963.

Lucius H. Pitts was in his second year as president of Miles College when all that happened. Many of his students were among the thousands who marched against segregation and discrimination, and he had a hand in the negotiated settlement that brought a temporary truce and an end to the demonstrations. In time the major civil-rights figures left Birmingham for other battlegrounds, and the reporters and cameramen followed. Lucius Pitts turned again to his primary mission: the rescue of a small and struggling college.

Miles had lost its accreditation in 1958 because of its poverty-level financing, a paucity of Ph.D.'s and an inadequate library. The Colored (now Christian) Methodist Episcopal Church, which had started the college soon after the turn of the century, wanted it to survive, and in 1961 the trustees turned to Pitts, an ordained minister in the denomination, and asked him to take the presidency. At the time, he was executive secretary of the Georgia Teachers and Education Association. He had a growing reputation as an outspoken young Turk in Atlanta's black community, and he was a thorn in the white flesh of the state education establishment. He was also a leader in the rising Southern integration movement, serving as vice president of the state NAACP and president of the Georgia Council on Human Relations.

Miles College, on the other hand, had little to offer him. A big salary cut and no job for his wife would cut their income in half; they and their four children would live in a rented five-room house. The college had about 750 students, a budget of $370,000, only one Ph.D. holder and an average faculty salary of $3,400 a year. Pitts was forty-six years old. He liked his chances in Atlanta, but he felt a deep commitment to his church, and after three months of indecision he took the Miles job because he was "forced by my own conscience to do it."

When I saw him there just before the fall term opened in 1969, Miles had 1,150 students, nine new buildings, a $2.75 million annual budget and a 65,000-volume library. Birmingham, too, had changed. George Wallace was no longer governor of Alabama—he aspired to a higher throne —and a Republican, George Siebels, was Birmingham's mayor. Dr. King was dead, and Reverend Abernathy, his successor as head of the Southern Christian Leadership Conference, seldom came to Birmingham. Reverend Shuttlesworth was pastor of a church in Cincinnati. Arthur Shores had been appointed in 1968 to the Birmingham City Council, and then had won the seat in a city-wide election. Bull Connor headed the Alabama Public Service Commission. Both the Kennedys were dead—slain, like Martin King, by assassins. Charles Morgan had gone to Atlanta, where he directed the Southern office of the American Civil Liberties Union. And A. G. Gaston had just been inducted into the Alabama Hall of Fame, along with nine other distinguished Alabamians, including—you guessed it—George Corley Wallace.

But for all the change, neither Miles nor Birmingham is out of the woods. Both the institution and the city are scarred by the past. President Pitts has an uncommon perspective of his college and its setting, and what he says about them helps to put his own profile in focus.

When I came here, I thought my involvement in civil rights was over. I came to work on the education of black people, preparing them to move through the doors being opened by the foot soldiers of the movement. The Georgia Teachers and Education Association was more than just an organization of Negro teachers—it was a civil-rights outfit.

Those were years when membership in the NAACP was a dangerous thing, yet we were their greatest source of support in Georgia. Unknown to others outside the profession, we collected dues for the NAACP, and our national organization, the American Teachers Association, gave a percentage of its income to the Legal Defense Fund.

In his various connections with the GTEA, the NAACP, the Georgia Council on Human Relations and the Southern Regional Council, Pitts had plenty of opportunities to fight segregation, and he gave much of his time to that effort. With a group of young Negro professionals in and around the Atlanta University complex he produced a booklet, *The Myth of Atlanta,* which documented racial discrimination in the city and said the old-guard Negro leadership was being duped by the white power structure. Through the GTEA he helped to expose racial inequality in the state's school system—with the undercover help of a few whites inside the school administration—and when he spoke out against the killing of Negroes in Terrell County, he was run out of "terrible Terrell," a rural county in the South Georgia black belt, and threatened by members of the Ku Klux Klan. A college presidency looked like a retreat from all that.

But the civil-rights movement was coming to full flower by 1961, and college students made up a large part of its following, not to mention its leadership. It was the year of the Freedom Rides, and when Edward R. Murrow came to town to do a television documentary called "Who Speaks for Birmingham?" a group of Miles students who wanted to be interviewed told their president they would march downtown if he didn't approve. "I knew a march would be murder at that tense time, so I told them to go ahead and be interviewed, and as a result of the program Miles got a drenching from the white community and from the black power structure too."

A selective buying campaign, again organized by students, was the next activity, and when Bull Connor retaliated by cutting out the entire county's food surplus program, the black community rallied behind the students and increased the effectiveness of the boycott. Connor later denied a permit to Miles for a door-to-door fund-raising campaign to get "a mile of dimes" for support of the library, so Pitts and the students called a press conference to put their plight before a larger audience.

"We got national publicity," he recalls, "and people found out we were here. More than 50,000 books have been sent to our library since then." Money came, too, in dribbles and chunks, and so did faculty applications and offers of volunteer help. "There is no end to the miraculous things which have happened," Pitts reflected. "We've gotten a great deal of good will from outside—and increased pressure from the white community of Birmingham. As a result of all this activity I became Peck's bad boy in this town. The white powers thought I was radical. In time we lost the support of almost all of them except Ed Norton. He had been on our board for twenty years, and he was independently wealthy and an honest man. He stayed with us until he died." Pitts added to his "radical" image in the eyes of many white Alabamians by becoming president of the Alabama Council on Human Relations and vice chairman of the state's advisory committee to the U.S. Civil Rights Commission.

President Pitts gave himself three years to get Miles reaccredited when he took the job in 1961, but when I visited with him in 1969 the college had been turned down twice and was facing its third try later that year. He had suffered a heart attack in 1964 and another seven months later, and worry over the school's future may have contributed to both. "We're more than up to standard now on the library and the faculty," he said, "but finance is still the critical problem. About 95 per cent of our students are from Birmingham, but most of our money other than tuition comes from outside the community. In spite of all we've accomplished, we face our worst crisis now, and it is financial. Half of our faculty could earn more teaching in the public schools. The local schools start new teachers at about $5,400, yet we've got people with master's degrees working for less than $5,000, and most of our Ph.D.'s get less than $7,000."

That must make the more than twenty people on the Miles faculty who now hold doctor's degrees among the lowest paid in the nation. It is just one of the economic crises hounding the school. An alumni association, now beginning to gain stability, chips in about $50,000 a year and promises to be an increasing source of support, but its contribution is less than 3 per cent of the college budget; the CME Church, with its own financial problems, can provide little more than that. Tuition and room and board are up to $1,400 a year—a stiff bite for Miles's none-too-affluent clientele—and while federal grants and loans help, they are never enough. And Pitt's own salary, after eight years on the job, is still less than he and his wife were making when they left Atlanta. "The board would gladly pay me more," he says, "but it would just throw things out of balance all along the line. I've got too many people with good offers elsewhere who stay here at heavy sacrifice."

With the people of Birmingham—whites especially, but Negroes too—giving inadequate support to Miles, the college has to depend on foundation and government grants to make ends meet, and Pitts points here to the root of the problem:

> It's a vicious circle—we can't get grants until we get accredited, and we can't get accredited without the financial support those grants would give us. If we can show that to the accrediting agency, I'm confident that the foundation support will be forthcoming.
>
> My view of Miles's role hasn't changed since I came here. This college has one of the greatest opportunities of any institution in the country to prove that gifted non-achievers— the great manpower waste in the black community, and in the white community too—can become contributing citizens rather than liabilities. Miles also has a great potential to be-

come a power base for black people in Birmingham, and possibly in the state—not only an academic power base but a means of providing interlocking relationships with other Negro-owned agencies and enterprises. Here in this metropolitan area, close to 4,000 black youngsters graduate from high school each year. No more than 15 per cent of them now go to college, and we get almost half of the ones who do. If we can prove that those who do go can make it, we can make a tremendous contribution. We're trying to make these young people aware of their own community—its inequities and its opportunities—so they can go out of here ready, knowing the value of political and economic power.

Ever since he came to Birmingham, Lucius Pitts has spoken his mind, and a lot of people, including some Negroes, haven't liked it. In 1963, *Time* magazine called him "the city's most respected Negro leader," and said he "has made Miles a school of faith, hope and distinction." Yet all the while, whites who had supported the college because they thought it would help them perpetuate segregation were being turned off by Pitts's bluntness. His home was one of the few places in town where an interracial social gathering could take place, he had run-ins with Bull Connor and Art Hanes and other elected officials, he got threatening telephone calls with monotonous regularity, and on several occasions the campus had to be cleared because of bomb threats. He has met George Wallace only twice—both times without any unpleasantness—but when a reporter in Seattle once asked him what he thought of the governor he replied that he hadn't come to Alabama to bury him, "but I would be glad to preach his funeral." That brought Pitts a lambasting in the Alabama press.

There are many things about the man that make him a complex figure. He is a middle-aged, middle-class Negro up from poverty, a country boy who went to the city and became a man. He is a preacher, an educator, a Southerner. He has stood on both sides of the generation gap, and has been labeled just about everything from an Uncle Tom to a black revolutionary. But the labels are hard to pin on him.

Pitts was born in rural Georgia, the seventh of eight children in a tenant farmer's family. His mother died when he was a child, but his father held the family together on pride, perpetual debt, and a common laborer's wages. Lucius was the first one to finish high school, and he made it to Paine College in Augusta for two years before an eye injury led to temporary blindness and forced him to quit. With good sight in only one eye—and with the insistence of his father, who came up with part of the money—he returned to Paine after three years, and graduated in 1941. Later he was a graduate student and an assistant to the dean of the chapel at Fisk University. He took a master's degree there and then preached and taught school and did youth work for about ten years. Then, in 1955, he went to Atlanta to become executive secretary of the GTEA.

That background, together with his experiences in Atlanta and Birmingham, has given him a determination to make Miles College strong and solvent, whatever the cost to his health or his "image." He has had opportunities to leave, but he stays, in his words, "because I have to. Accreditation has to come before I go—nothing but death would make me leave before then." At the same time, he says he is "reaching the point of diminishing returns as the president of this institution. We need a young, vigorous, trained educator and administrator, and I'm none of those—I'm a preacher."

The tough, continuous, uphill battle that Miles has had to fight in order to survive is not entirely a result of racial discrimination—many white liberal arts colleges are also in trouble these days—but race has played a big part, and Pitts sees it with the clarity of a black man who has felt the injustice of it:

> For a long time we had no relationship with the private white colleges in this town, but now they want a Negro or two at every function. They all want tokenism, but I'm not fooled by that. Birmingham is like many other cities: at the

point of economic and political power, there's no real seriousness about what's going to happen to the black man. Some
individuals are concerned, but for the most part what you
see are selfish interests or guilty consciences—and the latter
have no power. The people who *will* help can't, and those
who *can* help won't. I don't believe there is a serious desire
on the part of any major political figure in America at the
national level to *really* be concerned about moving the black
people into the mainstream, economically and politically. I
can understand and appreciate the rebellion of young people
in this country, in particular the black young people who
often cannot enunciate what they feel but who feel it, and
manifest their feelings the best way they know how.

I'm more knowledgeable about what's happening to us than
I was six years ago, and I believe that at the rate we're going,
the black man in twenty-five years will be farther behind
than he is now. In Birmingham, if you sent 10,000 people
downtown tomorrow, they'd let them march. There would be
no dogs or water hoses, there would only be promises, and
three weeks later they'd be operating just about like they
were before. It's like when I was a waiter. The man would
say, "Boy, this steak is too cold and too tough." So you take
it back, fling it on the stove, poke it with an icepick, put a
little parsley around it and take it to him again, and he says
"Yeah, that's fine." That's the way America is—the same old
thing, with just a little garnish.

The young people talk about Uncle Tom, but they don't
know their history very well. Tom didn't tell all he knew.
Today if you say you're going to burn this town down, police all over the country get mace and tear gas, and they tap
your phone lines and check on the movements of your leaders. They divide us by pulling off four or five top leaders,
putting one on the planning board, one on the water board,
one on the recreation board—but nobody on the school
board, or the finance committee, or the audit committee. They
have elections citywide instead of by districts, so we can't use
segregated housing as a weapon against them, and they change
the names of black schools when they're forced to integrate
them, and they won't use Negroes as curriculum directors or

as principals of desegregated schools. The way we're going, we'll end up like the New York schools—segregated, and with no black administrators. The businesses name vice-presidents for special marketing—and that means black marketing. The universities have assistant deans to handle black students. It's all by design, and you find the same thing wherever you look, whether it's in the Democratic party or the federal government.

And then there's Nixon and the so-called "Southern strategy." No, I'm not disillusioned. I was disillusioned a long time ago, but my eyes are open now. If I were ten years younger, I'd resign from Miles and become Carmichael and Brown and Newton all wrapped into one, in the field of education—a revolutionary, minus the violence and separatism. Somebody's got to tell the story. Somebody's got to be free enough to tell the foundations, "You go to hell, you're telling a lie," when they say they're for freeing the black colleges. Somebody's got to tell the U. S. Office of Education to look at the record and see that about one hundred institutions get something like 85 per cent of all the federal education dollars, and that only one black institution—Howard University—is on that list, and Howard is a child of the federal government. Black schools get about 3 per cent of the current federal support for higher education. Negro higher education is bankrupt. All we have to do is shake our heads and they'll fall off.

Somebody needs to tell them, he said, and he talked like a man who knew exactly what to say. A couple of months later, the more than one hundred predominantly Negro colleges in the country announced the formation of an organization to take their case forcefully to every potential public and private source of support. Lucius Pitts was one of the group's backers and spokesmen. Some whites, approaching paranoia about the threat of separatism, were deeply alarmed, but they missed the message.

Says Pitts:

I'm trying to find my way step by step in dealing with the idea of separatism. But I make it clear that I don't believe in it as an absolute philosophy. That would be impossible and impractical, like going to Mars on skis. It's a bad turn, a wrong direction, but more and more black students are learning, much faster than most of us, that violence and separatism is a no-win policy. Economic and political and educational power for blacks is a possible dream. We've got to get enough people who are educated and making money, people who won't build $150,000 houses in Beverly Hills just to be noticed, but who will put some of that money into economic power for people. We can harness the energy, the restlessness, and the native ability of young blacks so they recognize that their lives are tied to that kid in the ghetto. If white America—the power structure—hopes to save a modicum of this pseudo-democratic capitalist system, they'd better hear that. Their own young are disenchanted with the system, and they can shake the boat enough to turn liberals into moderates and moderates into ultra-conservatives. This country could be taken over by the Wallaces, and we'd have a bloodbath of ideology instead of race.

That isn't separatism talking. But such statements draw a widely mixed reaction, because Pitts won't let himself be typed as a separatist or an integrationist or any other kind of doctrinaire true believer. "By my own definition, I'm a militant," he says. I'd venture to say that most of the students here would call me a moderate. The more vocal ones could call me an Uncle Tom—including my own twenty-year-old son, who's probably at home stewing right now because I'm letting my supper get cold while I talk to another visiting white man." He smiled, and then added, "I've learned more from him in the last nine months than I learned in all the years I went to school." He went on:

Most of the white community would say I'm a radical. I think most middle-class Negroes would consider me a militant, and the same is true of most Negro churchmen. Some of the people on the street would agree, and the rest would say I'm a moderate. All of that bothers me, that business of labeling, because it simply means that we're divided. The success or failure of black people in Birmingham depends in large measure on our ability to develop understanding, trust, and unity. There are people in the white community who encourage this division. They're phony liberals who don't really care what happens to the Negro, and what they end up doing is driving wedges between black people, instead of bringing us together. And there are black phonies too—maybe I'm one. I have a wife and four children. Sometimes I rationalize my commitment. How much am I willing to pay for freedom and justice?

He didn't answer the question, but it is obvious that Pitts has already paid a heavy toll in terms of health, economic security, and peace of mind. He would not make a big thing of it; he would probably say he has got more than he has given, and that could be so. But he has surely carried more than his share, and the same would apply to most of the educators in the South's Negro colleges.

John Monro is a case in point. He is director of freshman studies at Miles, a white man, as it happens (more than one third of the Miles faculty is white), and until 1967 he was dean of Harvard College. Lucius Pitts lured him to Miles for a summer back in 1964, and while he was there got him turned on by the autobiography of Frederick Douglass. Monro came back for two more summers, and then left Harvard altogether because he was convinced that what was happening at Miles was more important.

Monro is no misdirected missionary, no bleeding-heart liberal. He's a direct and unpretentious New Englander, a man who believes in people and who loves to teach. He came to Miles at a time when the white man's welcome on the black campus was wearing thin, and when the curtain was falling on the Southern civil-rights scene, and he knew those things were happening. But Monro wasn't late; he wasn't looking for thanks, or for attention. Pitts says of him, "He's a strong man, with strong opinions freely expressed, yet it never gets personal with him. When Carmichael came here and gave his 'Honky go home' speech, Monro just laughed. He's introduced Malcolm X in his classes, and he agrees with Malcolm more than I do. About a fourth of our students wouldn't buy him when he came, but I'd say that's down to about 5 per cent now, and the more they get to know him, the better he'll be. He's been a breath of fresh air for Birmingham. One white man said of him, 'This man ain't no cracker—he's a nigger,' and he *is* black, in many ways." It was the ultimate compliment.

Some white academicians thought John Monro had taken leave of his senses when he went to Miles. They said it was a dead end, that the Negro colleges were on the decline, that many of them—especially unaccredited ones like Miles— would have to close. But Miles will be around for a long time, teaching kids the newly desegregated white colleges say are unteachable; and every time a youngster comes out of there with the tools and the cool to be competitive, people like Pitts and Monro know they're in the right place at the right time. On different occasions, both men had told me about one such student, a young man named U. W. Clemon, and I was going to see him the next day.

Before I left President Pitts, he talked about the South and where it fits in the latter-day search for racial justice.

> The South is worth saving. It could take the leadership in this nation in human relations easier than any other section of the country. It's like the old farmer said: "When you ain't never done nothin', you don't have to undo." The South hasn't done anything about real economic and political participation by its Negro citizens. So it's not a matter of departing from something; anything we do begins to show. If the South begins to make a serious effort it'll get happy inside, and find that it doesn't bring down calamity.

> There's something warm about Southerners. There's less duplicity than in other sections. Racism has been naked and undisguised here; it's been "Stay in your place," or "Here's poison, nigger—eat it and die, you black sonofabitch." In other parts of the country they've said, "Here's a piece of cake," but the poison is inside, and it stultifies and sterilizes

black people. The South can begin to realize that the black leadership in this country had its roots here, and the ones who leave are still Southern. If the South gives itself an opportunity, we can go on. We need some deaths—not violent ones, but some great big funerals—and they have to come soon and often. Ten good ones in this town in a year and Birmingham would move. I know some good men who want to move, but they're afraid of Daddy, who's still chairman of the board.

There's a tremendous potential in the South, but I'm very doubtful that we're going to see it soon enough. The economic power structure is too conservative, and it's sweeping the whole country, giving the South—giving George Wallace —more credibility. As big business and industry come South they get caught up in the conditioning that's already gone on. Wallace still runs Alabama, and people don't want to get involved in change. The rednecks, the political rednecks, are now using a different kind of skin cream. The same guys who used to say "Damn you niggers" now say "We're all gonna work together." They're learning to give a little rather than say "Never." They aren't fooling me.

The South is worth saving. It has a greater potential than New York or Ohio or Michigan. But I'm doubtful we'll have time.

*   *   *   *   *

"One U. W. Clemon is enough to justify the existence of Miles College," John Monro said. Pitts called him "one of the four or five most satisfying students we've had. He's not as well thought of among some of his colleagues here in town as he is on our campus, and most of the white lawyers are either afraid of him or hate his guts. He's too militant, too honest, too ethical."

Clemon was born not far from the Miles campus in Fairfield, one of the more than thirty incorporated towns in Jefferson County. Downtown Birmingham, eight miles to the east, was a world away. His father was a transplanted Mississippi sharecropper who worked as a laborer for the

Tennessee Coal and Iron Company, the giant subsidiary of U.S. Steel. "My father had the best of intentions," Clemon says, "but he was not one who managed his money or his affairs very well, so I came out of a matriarchal family." He was the sixth of nine children, and half a dozen times during his childhood his mother had to find them a new place to live because the rent money had gone for a bottle or a crap game. One of the places was in Dolomite, a rough and seedy company town. There, nine members of the Clemon family lived in a two-room house with no plumbing and no electricity. U. W. (the initials are his full name) started to school there, and did poorly.

When he was ten the family moved to Westfield, another company town. Things were better there (three rooms, electricity), and U. W.'s interest in school picked up. He was thirteen when the Montgomery bus boycott was beginning to attract national attention:

> It didn't make a big impact on me at first, but by the following year I was becoming very conscious of racial injustice, and that was when I started getting interested in the law. I was very naïve at that point. I didn't see the police as representing the law—lawyers and judges did that. I had heard of Demetrius Newton, a black lawyer who often represented people in the courts against the police at that time, and I thought that being a lawyer was the best way— maybe the only way—to protect the rights of people. I was quiet and withdrawn, and not athletic at all—though all my brothers were—and I read a lot. If I had been more outgoing, I probably wouldn't have developed the legal interest.

Several run-ins with the police also contributed to that interest:

> One day when I was about fourteen, two cops in a patrol car stopped several of us walking down the road. One of the cops pointed to one of my friends and said, "Come here, nigger." He got in the car and they drove off with him. When they brought him back a few minutes later, his pants were

soaking wet. They had made him urinate on himself. One of my brothers was stopped by the police once, and when he forgot to say "Yes sir" he got hit on the head with a billy club. Because of experiences like that, I haven't exactly felt generous toward the police. My mother had a lot on her, and she felt we should take things as they were with the police, say "Yes sir" and all that—it was the survival instinct in her —but I was hot-headed, and I didn't believe her. A couple of times I refused to say "Yes sir," and nothing happened. Looking back, I can see I was foolish to take that chance, because blacks and poor whites got beat up regularly by the cops.

Clemon graduated valedictorian of his class in Westfield in 1961, and after doing well on a national English examination he was offered a scholarship by Howard (now Samford) University in Birmingham. "It was the first time a Negro high school had been represented among the winners, and they didn't know I was black," he says. "When I called them about the scholarship, they told me they weren't accepting Negroes." Clemon wanted to go to Morehouse, and when he was offered a scholarship there he took it, but he withdrew after one semester because of a dispute over a physical education requirement: "Dr. Benjamin Mays, who was the president then, wrote me a letter saying I had done a very foolish thing in not honoring my scholarship. 'I'm afraid you'll live to regret this decision for the rest of your life,' he said. I took it all in stride, went on up to Miles and talked to Dr. Pitts, and got in there with a scholarship and no physical education requirement."

U. W. had participated in one or two sit-ins during his short stay in Atlanta, but for the most part he had been somewhat removed from civil rights. When he got to Miles in January 1962, things began to pick up:

Miles students were the only ones demonstrating in Birmingham at that time. Frank Dukes, who is now director of development at the college, was our leader. We had no affilia-

tion with any civil-rights organization, and the black minis-
terial association here opposed us—they thought we were too
radical. We had a selective buying campaign going, calling
for the removal of "white" and "colored" signs downtown
and the employment of Negro clerks and policemen. The
merchants agreed to remove the signs and promised to hire
Negroes. We presented the City Commission, headed by Bull
Connor, with 1,500 signatures on a petition asking for Negro
cops—the city had none at that time—and when I spoke at
our meeting Connor called me an outsider because I didn't
live in the city proper. He told me to shut up and sit down,
so another guy had to read the petition, after which Connor
adjourned the meeting and told one of his assistants to "get
some police and get these niggers out of here."

We told them the Southern Christian Leadership Conference wanted to come into Birmingham, but they didn't
listen. They didn't do anything. And that fall, SCLC held its
convention here. After Dr. King decided to open a campaign
in Birmingham the following spring, SCLC took over and our
group wasn't consulted any more. We were pushed aside and
had no official role in all that followed, but we stayed together as a group and took part in the marches.

Clemon marched half a dozen times in the big spring of
1963, but was never arrested. That summer he went to a
human-relations seminar in Indiana, sponsored by the National Student Association, and there he met for the first
time with white students active in the civil-rights movement.
The following summer he went to Nigeria on an Operation
Crossroads Africa project. "My family didn't want me to go,
and my friends thought I was crazy," he recalls. "Then,
nobody wanted to be identified with Africa."

In 1965 he graduated from Miles—again winning valedictorian honors. He had decided as a junior that he wanted to
go to Columbia Law School in New York, but he didn't
bother to apply until the day he finished college, and it took
intervention by President Pitts to get him in. He didn't like
New York at all—"too impersonal, too dirty"—and didn't

particularly care for the law school either, except for a few
professors whom he found "very approachable, helpful, and
interested in students." One of them steered him toward the
NAACP's Legal Defense and Education Fund, where he
was later to work as an intern.

But his first-year grades were pretty good, and tokenism
had come to Alabama. Samford University, which had refused him a scholarship five years earlier, now wanted him
to transfer there, and so did the University of Alabama.
Clemon went as far as writing to have his transcript sent to
Alabama, but the dean at Columbia wrote him a letter asking him to return, and Pitts and Monro persuaded him to go
back. He had had enough of New York, but he decided to
stick it out.

There followed a summer internship with the National
Labor Relations Board, and then he married his college
sweetheart and took her back with him for his last year.
U. W. worked for the Legal Defense Fund part-time that
year, and then stayed on as an intern there for four months
after his graduation. In October 1968, he and his wife returned to Birmingham to stay, and he is now a partner in
the law firm of Adams, Baker, and Clemon. In his office in
the Masonic Temple Building, he talked about New York
and Columbia, and his first year back home.

My black friends in law school thought I was conservative.
They issued a statement during the Columbia building seizure
charging the law faculty with racism. I convinced one or two
black students that we should put out a statement repudiat-
ing that charge, and we did. Most of the other black law students refused to speak to us. Out of 300 people in the class,
only ten of us were black, and only two—James Meredith
and I—showed up to get our degrees. Of the twelve black
students who started in law school with me, seven were from
the South, and I'm the only one who's come back. I guess I
am conservative by their standards. But I knew what I was
coming back to—this is a conservative town, and my actions

are seen as radical by the white community here. We've got a very long way to go. I'm regarded as the most militant black lawyer in this city. The radical blacks have to support me because I'm the closest any black lawyer comes to them. If I were in another city I'd have to contend with the separatist philosophy, but we don't have much of that here.

The city of Birmingham, with 400,000 people, is 42 per cent black, and the metropolitan area population, approaching 800,000, is 34 per cent black. There is one Negro, Arthur Shores, on the city council, and most of the city's boards and commissions also have token black representation. But the 600-man city police force has fewer than twenty blacks— none above the rank of patrolman—and all judges in the courts are white. There are about twenty Negro lawyers (only half of them in active practice), about eight black doctors, a dozen dentists, one architect, and perhaps fifteen struggling contractors. Roughly 85 per cent of all Negro children in the city school system were still in segregated schools at the end of 1969, and the other half-dozen school systems in Jefferson County had an even higher degree of segregation. No black candidates had come forward for the mayoralty or the legislature, and the legislature remained an all-white body. Birmingham and Alabama have indeed changed since 1963, but it is glacial, grudging change, and it has only just begun.

In that context, labels like "militant" and "conservative" are too relative to have any meaning. But whatever U. W. Clemon is called, he is as good an example of what has changed in Birmingham as you're likely to find. He and his two colleagues handle a large number of school-desegregation cases for the Legal Defense Fund. Clemon's case load is almost exclusively in the field of civil rights, particularly in school desegregation and police brutality suits. His prosecution of several brutality cases and an ensuing protest from a group of black community leaders—chief among them being L. H. Pitts—led to a grand jury investigation, and when the jury reported that it had found no concrete evidence of police brutality, Clemon said in a speech to the Jaycees that the investigation was a whitewash. After that, Police Chief Jamie Moore—he of the 1963 struggle—said he wouldn't tolerate brutal acts by his men, and with dramatic suddenness, complaints of mistreatment at the hands of the police diminished to near zero.

In school-desegregation cases, too, Clemon has been effective, operating with the confidence of a man who knows he is on the side of the law. When the Justice Department under John Mitchell deserted the Legal Defense Fund in the prosecution of school cases, Clemon objected that "the Nixon Administration position puts those of us who have been conservative in the eyes of the black militants in a very difficult position. We've said the legal processes will work, and now we're being slapped in the face with that." He said privately to a friend, "I've had faith in the judicial process up until now, but if the Nixon appointees gain a majority on the court, I don't know if it will be possible to keep that faith." Not long after that, the U.S. Supreme Court ordered thirty Mississippi school districts to desegregate immediately, in spite of a plea from the Justice Department for more time. It was the court's first major decision under its new Chief Justice, Warren Burger—himself the first Nixon appointee to the court—and the likelihood of a dramatic reversal of the desegregation decisions of the past fifteen years seemed very remote. The message seemed to be that even a Nixon court could not turn back the clock. Clemon read that message with great satisfaction— and then he got ready to take several school systems back into court, to be judged according to the new decision.

In 1963, Arthur Shores was a black lawyer in Birmingham handling civil-rights cases. What he sought for his clients seems in retrospect to have been modest, even conservative, yet for his audacity to challenge steel-ribbed segregation his home was bombed twice, his wife was injured, and his family

was terrorized. In 1969, Arthur Shores ran second in a field
of 25 to win one of the seats on the Birmingham City Council. That is change, hopeful but inconclusive evidence that
Birmingham might yet do justice to all its citizens. But what
has happened to Arthur Shores may be less significant than
this: a twenty-six-year-old black lawyer handling civil-rights
cases in Birmingham now is younger, more visible, more
militant, better trained, better supported, more effective, and
in less personal danger than his predecessor of seven years
earlier. That is what John Monro meant when he said one
U. W. Clemon is enough to justify Miles College.

Birmingham has changed, but it is still virgin territory for
the seekers of racial justice. "If this generation permits it to
be so, I'm sure we'll end up just like the North," Clemon
says. "But you see, it doesn't have to be so."

* * * * *

On December 3, 1969, the Southern Association of Colleges and Schools awarded full and formal accreditation to
Miles College.

Sarah Patton Boyle

Someone had written to ask her why she had "retired from the civil-rights front," and in her reply, Sarah Patton Boyle gave three reasons. "One was the shift in focus from the South to the big Northern cities. I know a great deal about the one, and nothing at all about the other." The second reason, she wrote, "was the shift in influence from whites to Negroes. When I first took my stand with Negroes against the white South, little attention was paid in the white press to anything a Negro said. . . . White spokesmen were greatly needed for the succees of the cause. This is no longer true. In fact, thank God, the reverse is true." The third factor in her decision was "the shift in interest from brotherhood to economic power. I certainly see the value of economic power but it does not appeal to me as a goal for whites and so naturally it does not appeal to me as a goal for Negroes. The concept of the brotherhood of man kindles me. I am willing to suffer and die to help us all approach the goal of the brotherhood of all men. I do not feel that way about a power struggle, whether between nations, or groups, or individuals. I was brought up to believe in the value of only one power, the power of love."

Then Mrs. Boyle closed her letter: "These three factors

combine to make almost anything I have to say concerning the present struggle quite irrelevant to most concerned ears. I always think it rather tragic when people fail to recognize their own irrelevance and continue to talk when they no longer have anything pertinent or effective to say. So I am not talking anymore. As the Bible says, 'There is a time to speak and a time to be silent.' I spoke when I thought it was time to speak. By the grace of God I hope to be silent now."

Mrs. Boyle's time to speak had come "like a bolt of lightning" in 1950, when a Negro student filed suit to gain admission to the University of Virginia. For fifteen years, she pursued her vision of brotherhood with all the zeal and devotion of a convert, which she was, and it is doubtful that any other middle-aged, white-skinned, blue-blooded Virginia lady was ever so transformed. Her commitment was total, and it was costly. In the middle of the 1960s, when the scene and the mood of the civil-rights movement shifted so dramatically, Mrs. Boyle became convinced that she had nothing more of value to contribute to it. Her time to be silent, she said, had come.

She has remained on the sidelines ever since, and like so many others who were deeply involved in the civil-rights cause, her name is no longer widely recognized and the memory of her contributions has faded. Patty Boyle is one of the unsung casualties of the war against white supremacy —one of the many. She is more fortunate than some, having found herself in the struggle, and she has no regrets about her involvement. Part of her story was told in *The Desegregated Heart,* the first of her two books, published in 1962. This is another part.

That Patty Boyle ever came to believe in human equality is a remarkable fact in itself, for she was indoctrinated from childhood in the belief that her family was superior—not only to Negroes, but to most white people. She was born near Charlottesville on the original plantation of her great-great-great-grandfather, who had been a general in the Army of the Revolution. One of her great-grandfathers served for a time as governor of Virginia, and her grandfathers served in the Confederate Army on the staffs of Stonewall Jackson, J. E. B. Stuart and Robert E. Lee. Her father, an Episcopal clergyman, was an executive in the national hierarchy of the church, and her mother's family background was equally as impressive. Patty and her sister, five years older, were the recipients of this rich heritage—they were descended from original white Americans, and they were raised to believe that nothing was more important than that fact. The heritage and traditions of the family were what mattered most, and good breeding was the key to it all. "It was like breeding dogs or horses," Mrs. Boyle recalls. "The best people in Virginia were supposed to observe the blood lines, and they did—they tended to meet, and marry, only each other. I believed that you inherited your traits of character, intelligence, manners, and sensitivity. I've put all this completely behind me now. It bores me extravagantly, except as an amusing memory, because I don't believe it anymore. I've met too many people who didn't even know who their grandparents were, yet they had all of the traits that I had been raised to believe came from breeding."

So strong was this sense of social superiority in Patty's parents that she and her sister were not sent to the public schools; they were tutored at home: "Public school was beneath us. We were 'better' than those people—all of whom were white, of course—and my mother was afraid I'd grow up and marry one of them." Her only formal education came much later, when she went away to art school.

The United States was the best place in the world, the South was the best of America, Virginia was the best of the South, and the Pattons and their elite companions in the upper class were the best of Virginia. They inherited the culture, the principles, and the snobbery of their forebears, and after the Civil War they inherited their debts as well. The resulting poverty was a relative thing; it was austerity on the heels of conspicuous affluence, not the empty, destitute poverty of the masses, and it was worn proudly by the aristocrats, like a badge of honor. And curiously mixed in with the austerity and the aristocracy were some characteristics which seemed at times to contradict the rest of Patty Boyle's education. There was the principle of *noblesse oblige*, the sense of responsibility for the welfare of the underclasses, and there were the principles of fairness, generosity, hospitality, courtesy, courage, honor. A sense of security and well-being dictated a faith in the essential goodness of people, a belief that underneath meanness and crudeness were often hearts of gold. And from all this came the aristocrat's perception of the Negro, a perception that Patty believed in and accepted without question for forty-four years.

Its essence was paternalism. You called them "nigras"— never "niggers"—and you expected them to lie and steal and cheat, because those were racial traits. You didn't approve of such behavior, but you usually didn't hold Negroes accountable for it—it was simply a manifestation of their primitive nature. You provided them a cabin to live in, and clothes to wear, and a little money, and when they got sick you brought the doctor, and when they died you sat in a pew up near the front at the funeral and your eyes brimmed with tears beside the grave. You loved them, the "good nigras"—they were simple and friendly and obedient, like your favorite pet. They knew their place, and of course they liked it; they were happy. That last point was especially important to the white aristocrat's perception of his darkies, his good nigras: they approved of your condescending love, of being treated as underlings. They *had* to be poor, dumb and happy, because the whole stereotype was supported by that belief.

"I kept a childlike image of Negroes long after I ceased

to be a child," Mrs. Boyle recalls. "I saw them as culturally immature, and of course as socially inferior; but like Kipling's Gunga Din, they were somehow purer in heart, more faithful, more true than whites. Until I was twelve, I was largely in the care of Negro adults, and some of my playmates were Negro children, and I loved them." After that, her parents took over. Formalities were imposed, "status" and "place" ruled her relationships, condescension became required. Segregation took over. Patty bridled a bit at first, and sometimes she broke the new taboos, but when her indoctrination was over she was a typical Southern lady—polite and gentle, noble and generous, and convinced that a special love and understanding existed between people like her—people of class—and their nigras.

She went to Washington for a while to study art, and then returned to Charlottesville to live with her parents and take occasional courses in the summer school at the University of Virginia. There Patty met Roger Boyle, a young man from a proper Maryland family, and in 1932, when she was twenty-six, she married him. Boyle went on to become a professor of speech and dramatic art at the university, and for almost twenty years they lived quietly in the insulated and remote atmosphere of high-key culture and low-key aristocracy that is the University of Virginia. They also lived providently, in the comfortable and complacent style of that time and place, and they raised two sons, and Mrs. Boyle became moderately successful as a writer of non-fiction articles for magazines. In such a setting, race and place were not conscious concerns; they were taken for granted.

In the summer of 1950, a young Negro named Gregory Swanson went to court to challenge the Commonwealth of Virginia's law—and the University of Virginia's practice—of racial segregation. Swanson, a lawyer from Danville, wanted to pursue further study in the university's law school, and he had the backing of the National Association for the Advancement of Colored People. Patty Boyle was shocked, then fearful, then guilt-stricken: "It was like a bolt of lightning. I'd never really thought about this issue before. Swanson obviously was well qualified, and this was Thomas Jefferson's university. It hit me all of a heap."

In a year's time, Gregory Swanson had come and gone without incident, apparently having got what further education he wanted, but the education of Patty Boyle had just begun. At the news of Swanson's coming—and with her husband's approval—she started a one-woman campaign of letter-writing and poll-taking and buttonholing to promote his acceptance. With complete sincerity and the best intentions, she laid her maternalism and her romanticized and unconscious racism before Swanson. "Be grateful—*visibly* grateful—" for whatever you get, she coached him. She said it was "the time for gratitude, not more pushing," and she warned that trying to move too fast "will only lose what's already been gained." She wrote a free-lance article called "We Want a Negro at the University of Virginia," and when she showed it to Swanson and he asked incredulously if she really intended to try to have it published, she replied modestly, "Please don't feel grateful, Gregory. I feel privileged to help."

In her slow and painful awakening to the injustices done to Negroes, Mrs. Boyle believed that her public support of desegregation would initially be applauded by most Negroes and opposed by most whites. Not surprisingly, the Negro support was slow in coming; those who were not either insulted or frightened by her remarks may simply have doubted her sincerity. But most of her white friends gave her praise and encouragement—privately—and open opposition from whites was negligible. Mrs. Boyle believed that the vast majority of white Southerners, once they had been awakened to the injustice of segregation, would abandon it willingly. *Brown vs. Board of Education* was still four years in the future.

Trying to do what she thought was right, Mrs. Boyle

stumbled naïvely from one blunder to the next. She read the white expressions of support as the general feeling of most whites, and her opinion sampling in Charlottesville and in the university community confirmed her belief. She misunderstood—and was misunderstood by—the Negro community time after time. Instead of the love and appreciation she expected, she got suspicion and hostility. She became bewildered and resentful, and then T. J. Sellers rescued her.

Sellers was the editor of Charlottesville's Negro newspaper. Mrs. Boyle went to him for help, and on the condition that she not approach it as "a white lady slumming," he "enrolled" her as his only student in the "T. J. Sellers course for backward Southern whites." For several months she visited his office weekly, and he introduced her to a perception of Negroes that bore no resemblance to the blinkered paternalism she had grown up with. She recalls that experience: "He is an extraordinary man. No matter how exasperated he became with me, he never lost his capacity to see the other side. He could hear me, even when he was angry. He attacked my ignorance, my ingrained attitudes, and my unconscious habits, and I began to see for the first time how we had denied the Negro his humanity, and how I had been a part of that." Later, she wrote a regular column for his paper.

In 1951, Mrs. Boyle started a letter-writing campaign to promote the cause of integration, writing not only for herself but for about a dozen others who signed her compositions and sent them to the newspapers. She also wrote book reviews and free-lance articles, and built up a busy speaking schedule. What she had learned from Sellers made her less blunder-prone, but her message remained essentially unchanged: "I wanted white and colored Southerners to love one another and thus bring the Southern dream true." She still believed that most of the injustice and cruelty which Negroes suffered resulted from unconscious and unintended acts by whites who did not realize how prejudiced they were, and she wanted to explain those whites to Negroes, and explain Negroes to whites. She saw herself as a catalyst, a reconciler; and she lacked none of the confidence or the courage to sustain her crusade. As events were to show, what she lacked was a real understanding of the protagonists whom she sought to reconcile.

Sellers moved to New York in 1953, and until late in 1954 Mrs. Boyle's faith in the inherent good will of the white Southerner remained intact. She circulated petitions for the removal of "whites only" signs, continued writing letters and articles and making speeches, kept calling on political and religious and civil leaders to speak out for an end to segregation. Not many voices were heard, but her audiences were receptive and her friends continued their encouragement, and more and more Negroes ended their initial silence and gave her support. Then came 1954:

> Until the Brown decision, I believe people were willing and ready to accept integration. I took lots of opinion samples among all income levels, and I was convinced that no more than 6 or 7 per cent of the people were unalterably opposed; the rest were willing, and had they been led by good people, we'd have been okay. But within six weeks after the decision, it was as though a door had been slammed shut. I had every reason to be optimistic until then, but the politicians took over, and the church failed, and the papers failed. It became hard to keep my faith in the South.

The following November, a public hearing was called by a special commission on public education which had been appointed by the governor to chart the state's course in response to the Supreme Court ruling. The course the commission ultimately chose was massive resistance, and the hearing itself was another sober lesson in Patty Boyle's education. It lasted fourteen hours, and the segs had a field day. Of the first ninety-three witnesses, only six whites—including Mrs. Boyle—and thirteen Negroes spoke in favor of integrating the schools. Members of the state's legislature led the opposition, and in their defiance of Negroes and the Supreme Court they spared no insult.

Mrs. Boyle recalls:

> It was one of the bitterest disillusionments of my life. I was the only person from Charlottesville who spoke in favor of integration. As far as I know, no one from the university even attended. I knew that the faculty there was liberal, and polls had shown that they favored change, yet not one of them spoke up, even though the state itself was requesting opinions. Who could more properly speak for freedom and equality than professors at Mr. Jefferson's university? Who could more justifiably speak concerning the future of Virginia's schools than the educators at our highest institution of learning? But when the time came to stand and speak, they were silent. They would only give private lip service to integration.

Now, sixteen years after that hearing and twenty years after Gregory Swanson broke the line, there are still not many more than one hundred Negroes at the University of Virginia.

Faith dies slowly in the true believer. Her optimism was shaken, but Mrs. Boyle clung to the belief that the white South would see the light: "I thought I was a spokesman for a large group of liberal whites in Charlottesville, and it never crossed my mind that they wouldn't stand up and be counted. There were some eloquent spokesmen in the Negro community, including Mr. Sellers, until he moved away. That same fall I sold an article to the *Saturday Evening Post*. It appeared the following February, and that's when the sky fell."

The Post titled the article, "Southerners Will *Like* Integration," and they played it big. The theme was Mrs. Boyle's belief in the South. She wrote:

> I do not claim that the whole story of Southern racial prejudice is a myth, but I do stoutly maintain that it is vastly exaggerated in our own minds, as well as in those of outsiders.

A few emotional individuals bellow threats and hatred, a few sensation lovers join them in the din, and the large majority, composed of good-willed but easygoing and peace-loving citizens, cower back, mistakenly assuming that there is nothing they can do about it because their "number is so small."

Our chief need, I think, is for the realization that if we believe in justice and equality for all, we are not only on the side of right but also on the side of the majority, and that we shall suffer no loneliness in our community if we stand up to be counted for what we believe.

By the time the article appeared, Mrs. Boyle was already suffering loneliness for standing up in her community, and the worst was yet to come. Hate mail followed, and insults, and threats. She was vilified in the letters-to-the-editor columns. The governor and the president of the university received letters demanding that her husband be fired, and a bill was even introduced in the legislature for that purpose. A few of her friends whispered their sympathy, and several Negroes wrote, called or wired her, but no whites defended her publicly:

My white friends ran for cover—including those who had applauded me loudest. The segregationist tide was running, and all over the South, public officials sounded like hoodlums, clergymen like bad little boys, liberals like goldfish. My sons agreed with me, though they were still young. My husband was distressed by the play given to the article in the *Post,* but even though it pained him, he didn't ask me to stop what I was doing. I was not the only white liberal in Charlottesville, but at that time I was the only one speaking out consistently.

She joined the local NAACP chapter, and her invitations to speak increased and spread outside the state, but her audiences were no longer white: "I believed intellectually that I could still influence whites," she now says, "but I didn't believe it emotionally any more. What kept me going was the growing trust of the Negro community. I couldn't let them down—there were so few white Southern voices. I couldn't let the attacks on Negroes go unchallenged."

In the summer of 1956, a six-foot cross was burned in the front yard of the Boyle home: "The general white reaction to that was to consider me responsible. It was as though I had brought it on myself by doing something I shouldn't have done. The Virginia Council on Human Relations had been organized by then, and I was vice president of it, but soon after the local chapter was formed they wanted to be 'moderate' and I was 'extreme' and an embarrassment to them. I was no longer a front-rank soldier with an unseen regiment behind me. I was a lone sniper in a tree."

Through the rest of the 1950s, Mrs. Boyle's ties among Negroes were strengthened while her white connections continued to drop. She received awards and citations from the NAACP, the Southern Christian Leadership Conference and several other Negro organizations. She continued to maintain in articles and speeches that she had "faith in God and a vast and unshakable faith in man," and she insisted that she wouldn't retire, but the strain of ostracism and rejection was severe, and she was getting tired. She went away to Koinonia Farm, the interracial cooperative farm in Georgia, to relieve the pressure and seek a fresh perspective, but the pressure was still there when she returned.

She recalls:

> The situation had become very painful for my family. My brother-in-law was treasurer of the local chapter of the Defenders of State Sovereignty and Individual Liberty, and my sister was very active in the Daughters of the American Revolution, and I was an embarrassment to them. Stringfellow Barr, the historian, who is my first cousin, was the only member of my family who approved of what I was doing—except my young sons, of course. My husband agreed with the principles I was fighting for, but he wasn't a crusader.

In the fall of 1959, the Charlottesville schools began to desegregate under a court order, and the occasion passed peacefully. Mrs. Boyle had already started on her book, *The Desegregated Heart,* and she worked on it steadily for the next two years. It was published late in 1962, and she resumed a limited involvement in civil-rights activities while working on her second book, *For Human Beings Only.*

"Things had changed when I became active again," she says. "Negroes didn't want white people explained to them any longer—they wanted results. They didn't care anymore whether whites meant well." She joined demonstrations in Richmond, Washington, and Charlottesville, and in June of 1964, at the request of Dr. Martin Luther King, she went to St. Augustine, Florida, to join a protest march.

On the dust jacket of *The Desegregated Heart,* Dr. King had called it "a great book . . . one of the most eloquent and captivating documents that has emerged from the Southern situation." He and Mrs. Boyle had met and talked on several occasions, and he knew her to be a committed apostle of racial equality and nonviolence, and when he asked her to join in the St. Augustine demonstrations and to go to jail for the cause, she went.

Arriving in St. Augustine by bus in the heat of the afternoon, she was met by a white teenager and taken to the local headquarters of the demonstrators. The conflict there concerned access to public accommodations, among other things, and had been in progress for several weeks. Organized white groups had attacked the marchers on several occasions, and the police, instead of preventing such attacks, had sometimes participated in them. Arrests and casualties were running high, and so was tension.

There was a rally at a Negro church that night, at which the Rev. Andrew Young, one of Dr. King's top lieutenants, sought twenty volunteers willing to join the 185 demonstrators already in jail. Mrs. Boyle was one of the volunteers. A march to the old slave market in St. Augustine followed the meeting, with state and local police and their leashed dogs surrounding the marchers, but the night ended without incident. After breakfast the next morning, Mrs. Boyle and four Negro teenagers were driven to within a block of the Monson Motor Lodge and were told to go and seek service in the motel's restaurant. Mrs. Boyle had expected to follow someone else's lead, but she found herself, as the only adult, serving as the small group's spokesman.

A waitress in the restaurant saw them coming and rushed to lock the door. The manager called the police, and within minutes the little knot of marchers was surrounded by reporters, television cameras, and the law. They were arrested, charged with "disturbing the peace, trespassing with malicious intent, and conspiring to commit a felony." At the jail they were put in segregated cells, Mrs. Boyle joining five other white women, and in the adjoining cell were twenty-seven Negro teenagers. Dr. King, who had been arrested earlier, was in a cell upstairs. More than two months earlier, Mrs. Malcolm Peabody, the seventy-two-year-old mother of the governor of Massachusetts, had spent two nights in the same jail after being arrested at a restaurant with a biracial group.

Allowed her one phone call, Mrs. Boyle tried to call home, but there was no answer, and she was not permitted to try again. Three days later she was bailed out, and that evening attended a rally at which the Rev. King spoke—he also having been released from jail. Late that night she got a ride to the bus station, and stood on the street in the dark waiting for the last bus. It came, late but finally, and she left St. Augustine for Virginia with a mixed feeling of relief and despair.

When the voter registration campaign opened in Selma, Ala., in the first month of 1965 and built to the climactic march to Montgomery in March, Mrs. Boyle was ill and hospitalized with an undiagnosed lung ailment. Cancer was suspected. Earlier, she had joined the Negro Episcopal church in Charlottesville "because none of the clergymen at the white church would stand up," and when she entered the hosptial she insisted on—and got—a room shared with a Negro patient. "I told them most of my visitors would be black, so there was no way integration could be escaped."

The ailment, though never diagnosed, turned out not to be serious. Patty Boyle's sixtieth birthday passed, and her despair deepened over the growing solitude of her personal life and the growing militance of the civil-rights movement. She felt alienated from all she had fought for, and she was weary:

> I couldn't be effective any more. The time for explaining and interpreting whites and Negroes to each other and increasing their understanding of one another seemed all over, and I felt I couldn't support the new tactics. What led me to become involved in the first place may be common to most Southerners who became involved in the movement: I had a deep and true love of Negroes—however much they may laugh at that. I had my wild stereotypes at first, and I was very naïve, and I'm sure many Negroes would say it was the stereotypes I loved, but my devotion was on a deeper level than that. The love I felt was often misinterpreted, sometimes because of my own inability to communicate it clearly. Some people read sex into it, or exploitation, or sickness, but it was none of those. It was a deep sense of brotherhood. It took me a long time to see fully what my instincts must have been telling me in 1950, but when at last I really saw the injustice, when I saw how we really had betrayed these people, I had no choice. I was totally committed to the brotherhood of man, and no price was too high for me to pay to help bring it into realization. How could I regret it now? How could I have done anything else? I have always believed in total commitment—I have to be sure I'm right about something before I can write or speak about it effectively—and I was sure I was right about the brotherhood of man, and about the moral underpinning of the Movement. When the original idealism of the revolution began to dissipate, I ceased to be creative. I was suddenly terribly tired. I just

can't give myself to what the Movement seems to me now to have become—one which is prepared to use any means, provided only that it works.

After James Meredith was gunned down while walking along a Mississippi highway in June 1966, Mrs. Boyle went to join the march that rose up in the wake of the shooting, and that was her last demonstration:

> The whole atmosphere had changed. This was not something I could die for any more. I had been warning whites that the adamant refusal to yield an inch to the Negro rights movement would bring on despair and then violence. I went to Mississippi to see whether this change in spirit had actually taken place, and it had. The whole atmosphere of the thing had changed. Dr. King was helpless and discouraged. Many of the marchers were no longer trying to sublimate their hostility. They would taunt the bystanders, provoke them deliberately. There was dishonesty and subterfuge and deception, and a general sort of moral disintegration. I saw nothing to live or die for in it.

It was on that march that Stokely Carmichael became the spokesman for a new movement of militant young blacks, and it was there that the "black power" slogan echoed across the civil-rights front.

Earlier, Mrs. Boyle had said she would never retire from the Movement, but so much had changed, and when she felt herself no longer to be in harmony with it, she had the honesty to say so. "A time to speak, and a time to be silent."

In 1965, after the second of their sons had finished his undergraduate work at the University of Virginia, the Boyles were divorced, and Patty moved to Arlington. The following year, when she gave up her commitment to the Movement, all she had left was her religious faith:

> My religion through all this was simply a personal relationship with Christ. After the cross was burned, everywhere I looked I saw nothing but evil and horror and hopelessness

and ugliness and disillusionment. Jesus Christ and the Christian faith were the only things lovely to look at that I could see, and they were enough. The church was helpful but not necessary for this. I never was active in church work, but I felt called upon to carry the banner for what the Christian faith stands for. I had to have a real and personal relationship with a personal God when so many other personal relationships were being destroyed. I still believe that if we are compelled to look upon injustice we will eventually remedy it, but I no longer believe that there is inherent goodness in all men. Genuine goodness comes and goes in people, and you can't depend on it being there in any given individual at any given time. God's invasion of us is what brings goodness.

In the concluding section of *The Desegregated Heart,* Mrs. Boyle describes her search for a personal relationship with God at the end of the 1950s, when she felt she had "nothing to give others anymore, and there was nothing I wanted from them." In that period of solitude she apparently found what she was looking for, and the religious experience she relates in the book reads like the discovery of a God outside man, almost as an alternative to man. The discovery was her main source of strength all through the 1960s—and apparently it still is.

With the same sense of certainty that kept her involved in civil rights for fifteen years, Mrs. Boyle now says she has no regrets about that involvement or about ending it, but she laments the circumstances which led her to retire:

I believe the mood and the strategy of the movement changed at the very time when they were beginning to win. Dr. King's methods had won over the opinionmakers, and given time, they would have won the people over. People were being educated to change their minds. Enough people were passionately concerned to make great change take place. I believe this nation could have been redeemed by the Negro people. I can understand *why* they despaired, but it was doubly tragic that they despaired just when they did. I understand their despair, and violence, and separatism—they have had provocation for all three—but I can't support violence and separatism. I think they are wrong.

In one of her few public expressions on civil right since 1965, Mrs. Boyle and John Howard Griffin, author of *Black Like Me,* published an exchange of their letters in a 1968 issue of *The Christian Century.* In those letters she had "no hope that anything of what we once envisioned can happen now." She criticized white liberals—perhaps the same ones whose silence had supported the white segregationist cause —for condoning black violence as a necessary thing "to prove their manhood to themselves" and to "get the frustrations out of their system." She said she wept "for the enormous failure of the Christian church. Having offered no support to the revolutionaries when they were altogether right, the church now in many places is giving both endorsement and support to the revolutionaries when they are no longer right." Saying she understood "with guilt and shame" the reasons for the new aims and methods of black revolutionaries, she added that denying black Americans responsibility for their own moral decisions "would be paternalism rising, more subtle but as ugly as before." Then she wrote: "I think it is the last insult to their manhood if we say to them, 'We chose evil but you couldn't help yourself.' Either both groups have free will or neither has. . . . I will not insult my black brothers by saying they had no choice. Nor will I insult them by endorsing for them a standard that I reject for us. . . . How insulting can we get?"

In the last of the letters to Griffin, Patty Boyle said Dr. King's Poor People's Campaign, then being planned, was "a stroke of genius. . . . And so I have hope again. . . . Hope is not in itself the answer. Love is the answer But hope enables us to seek the answer"

A month later, Dr. King was dead, shot from ambush by a white Southerner. "The brotherhood of man was more possible in the South twenty years ago than in any other part of the country," Mrs. Boyle said in a conversation after King's death. "There was a common experience among blacks and whites, an inward weaving together of the spirit that had the potential of transcending all of the evil that existed on the surface. But there is a loss of love now, and that advantage the South once had is rapidly disappearing. The South may become much worse than the North—as the North believes it already is."

She was talking about the South she once loved. It would do the right thing, she had thought, once the people are shown, once they see the light.

Patty Boyle is sixty-four years old now, and she is resilient. "I've become very much aware that the current oppressed minority is the aged," she says. "I've been doing some work in a retirement community, and there and elsewhere I see the elderly treated without a ray of respect. Their opinions are not listened to—they are like non-persons. The youth movement is anti-elderly, at least by implication. This is my new focus. Maybe I'll write about it." There is a sparkle in her eye, and a hint of indignation in her voice.

John Howard Griffin

In the literature of the civil-rights era, *Black Like Me* is on a shelf by itself. It would be arbitrary to call it the best book of the period—who could really rank such a diverse body of writings, anyway?—but it is probably the best seller (over 3½ million copies), and in the style and circumstances of its telling, it is one of a kind. *Black Like Me* is the journal of a white Texan who changed the color of his skin and made a six-week trip through the Deep South; it has not been unheard of for light-skinned Negroes to pass for white, but few whites have ever passed for black, and none of them has ever written about it the way John Howard Griffin did in *Black Like Me*.

The book belongs to the time when it was written. It was a personal documentation of white inhumanity to Negroes—a damning exposure of some whites, a shaming revelation to others, and a public confirmation of what Negroes knew from bitter and agonizing experience. In 1960, such a story needed telling, and it stirred hopes that the indictment it carried would be answered by a new commitment to justice on the part of fair-minded white Americans.

Now, a decade later, racial estrangement has grown

deeper. *Black Like Me,* far from spawning a new commitment to justice, is now a small volume among many, one of the unheeded warnings against a contagious sickness. Complacency and the sword can subdue the pen.

Black Like Me catapulted John Howard Griffin to prominence. He made the newsweeklies and network television and *The Reader's Digest,* he was vilified by segregationists and lionized by liberals, he received numerous human relations awards. With the passing of time that prominence has faded, but Griffin's name and the title of his book remain coupled in the public mind. He is the white man who turned black, or as a young inmate in a Michigan prison once described him, "the chuck who made himself into a splib."

There is more to Griffin than *Black Like Me.* He is an extraordinary man, a complex and at times mystical individual whose life has been marked by physical affliction and self-enforced solitude. In the years before 1960 his experiences were anything but typical, and since then he has remained an enigmatic person.

Griffin was born in Dallas in 1920 and grew up in Fort Worth, where his father was in the wholesale grocery business. His father came from an arch-segregationist family of Georgia Griffins—Marvin Griffin, one of the most unreconstructed of Georgia's ex-governors, was a distant cousin— but John's father was born in Texas, and he joined the Episcopal Church and left race-baiting behind him.

As a youngster, John Howard became deeply interested in science and music, and when he was fifteen he persuaded his parents to let him go to a boys' school in France to pursue his scholastic interests. In the five years he spent there he progressed rapidly through the lycée and into preparation for a career in medicine. He also experimented with the use of sound—in particular, Gregorian chant—as therapy for patients in a mental hospital, and in the process made musicology a parallel pursuit. The Catholic Church and its monastic orders became another intellectual interest of his during that time, and photography fascinated him too, and he pursued all of these eclectic concerns energetically.

When war spread across Europe, Griffin became active in a French underground effort to smuggle Jewish families out of Germany. By 1940 much of Europe was in Nazi hands, and Griffin returned to Texas, from where he joined the Army Air Force soon after Pearl Harbor. In 1945 he was injured in a bombing raid in the Dutch East Indies, and after a period of unconsciousness it was discovered that the severe head injury he had sustained had virtually destroyed his sight, leaving him with only faint perception. After being discharged he returned to Texas, legally blind but able to function with the aid of special low-vision lenses, and soon afterward he went to France again, hoping somehow to salvage some part of his plans for a medical career. A brain specialist there told him that his injury had made total blindness a certainty for him, and Griffin turned to the study of music, a pursuit that would not be foreclosed by the loss of sight.

By May 1947 his vision was gone, and he went back to Texas to live with his parents, who had moved to a farm near Mansfield, not far from Fort Worth. He studied in a school for the blind and later with a special teacher in New Orleans, and in 1949 he began writing. His first novel, *The Devil Rides Outside,* was published in 1952, and that same year he became a convert to Catholicism. In 1953 he married a young Mansfield girl who first came to his home as a piano student, and from then until 1957 he wrote another novel, *Nuni,* and studied philosophy and theology under the specially prepared long-distance tutelage of French theologian Jacques Maritain and other European friends of his. His wife, Elizabeth Ann, gave birth to the first two of their four children, and in January of 1957 a successful brain operation in Fort Worth restored his sight.

Griffin was then thirty-seven years old. No aspect of his

life had been ordinary. It had been a succession of contrasts —Texas and France, nominal Protestantism and devout Catholicism, sight and blindness—and it had been made more unusual by his diverse intellectual interests, his European interludes, the generally poor state of his health, and the style and intensity of his writing. Literary critic Maxwell Geismar called Griffin's first book "among the three best novels of the decade 1950 to 1960," and he said Griffin was "a mystic and religious writer" and a "powerful new talent in this country—a talent which is still largely ignored by the prevailing literary establishment in the United States." Into his dark and perplexing books and stories Griffin kneaded elements of the theology, philosophy, literature, and music he had become absorbed in since his first stay in France, and added to these the perceptions of a man who sees nothing, and thus sees all.

Blindness was responsible for much of what John Howard Griffin was and what he did in the intellectual and literary realm. It was also the thing which turned him to the study of racism and to the writing of *Black Like Me*. These are his recollections:

My childhood was Southern in the old sense, the terrible sense. We were not rich but not poor either, we were genteel Southerners, and I was taught the whole mythology of race. I had the black mammy, the summers in the country; the kind, Southern, slaveowner mentality was drilled into me, and veneered over with paternalism. We were taught to be good and kind, and we were given the destructive illusion that Negroes were somehow different. That Negro mammy overwhelmed us with love, and we never wondered who took care of *her* children, or saw anything wrong with her going back to that absolute pigpen to sleep. My parents were horrified at lynching—I remember their shame and dismay after a particularly brutal one in Waco when I was about seven— but in a way we were practicing slavery every day.

When I went to France as a boy I took a lot of that attitude with me. Then slowly, as I came to know African students from the colonies and then became involved with the Jewish victims of Hitler's racism, I began to discover how deep these patterns were and how profoundly I was damaged by them. But it was more an intellectual realization than an emotional or personal one—I still rationalized my racism. Then and later, religious faith influenced my developing consciousness. The study of music, of the chants, led me to a fascination with monastic systems, and my association with Jacques Maritain and Gerald Vann in France—Vann was a noted British theologian—and then Thomas Merton in this country coaxed me out of the agnosticism I had drifted into and led me eventually into the Catholic Church. It was those men who were chiefly responsible for my theological and philosophical studies during the years when I was blind, and Maritain is the godfather of my oldest child.

So I had this sort of intellectual, theological interest in racism when I became blind, and the loss of sight gave that interest a new dimension. Those last months of sight were agonizing, but also terrifying; my perception became so impaired that a shadow passing between me and the light made me flinch. The total darkness came as a kind of relief, because it was less of a frustration to be able to see nothing than it was to tell light from total darkness and nothing more, no shapes, no forms. The recovery of sight was, if anything, more terrifying than the loss of it. I had very light perception at first, and then rapid recovery, but my eye muscles had atrophied, and my eyes wouldn't be still, they moved around wildly, unable to focus. I couldn't stand it at first; I had to shut my eyes and return to the familiar. It took several months for me to return to normal.

It was during this time of blindness that racism became a preoccupation. I was overwhelmed by it. My past experiences, my religious encounter, and my academic studies came together with the personal experience of blindness, and the evil of racial discrimination was revealed by all of that in such a way that it struck me a tremendous blow. As a blind man, I couldn't tell black from white. Speech patterns, I learned, are regional, not ethnic. It was the sight of a man that made us discriminate, it was the hue of his skin. We had drawn up an indictment against a whole race of people. This absurd stereotype, this national abuse of sight, was devastating to me. And later, when I could see again, it was made manifest to me in another way, in the dehumanized hardness of the hate stare. The eye can reveal so much. We were told that only "white trash" had this irrational hatred, but these patterns are learned early by all kinds of men, men who can be rational on any subject but race. We were saying we judged men as individuals, yet at these profound levels we were judging by pigment.

While he was still blind, Griffin began to study racial conflict in the South, and soon after his sight was restored he started an investigation of the suicide rate among Southern Negro males. Many Negroes refused to answer his questions, and one of them finally told him, "The only way you can *know* what it is like is to wake up in my skin." The question had dogged him for years: What is it really like to be a Negro in the Deep South? He decided to try to find out.

Black Like Me tells the story. On November 1, 1959, he went to New Orleans. Under the direction of a dermatologist, he began to take large doses of a drug which darkens the pigmentation of the skin, and supplemented that with ultraviolet rays from a sunlamp and applications of a dark stain, like theatrical makeup. He also shaved his head. Within a week, he was very dark. And for the next six weeks, he walked and rode the bus and hitchhiked in Mississippi and Alabama and Georgia. He was a Negro, a black man, a nigger.

In *Black Like Me,* and in some additional entries in his journal which were published in 1968 for the first time in *The John Howard Griffin Reader,* it is clear that as a white man, Griffin had had no conception of the psychological and physical destructiveness of segregation and white supremacy. His journal describes the step-by-step exposure of a sensitive human being to an enormous evil he had only dimly perceived. It is one white man's vivid description for other white men of hell on earth, told as only one who had been there could tell it. Negroes did not need to hear the story; they lived it, and many still do, every day. And they have told it: Langston Hughes and Ralph Ellison and James Baldwin and countless others before and after them have told the story of *Black Like Me*. As the man told Griffin: "The only way you can *know* what it is like is to wake up in my skin." Whether reading Hughes or Ellison or Baldwin—or for that matter, Griffin—has given white Americans a true grasp of the enormity of the evil is impossible to say. Maybe the only way *is* to be black. If so, Griffin may be the only white man who knows.

And he could not stand it very long. After a month, he stopped the medication and relied on daily applications of the stain, passing back and forth from the black world to the white for another two weeks. Finally, he went back home, taking with him a profound respect for his black brothers and a deep sense of shame and humiliation for his white ones. The book followed—serialized first in *Sepia* magazine —and then there were television appearances and interviews and a flood of letters (most of them favorable). And after that there were some anonymous threats, and Griffin was hanged in effigy on the main street of Mansfield, and his parents, who had supported him, got the silent treatment and the hate stares right along with Griffin and his wife.

They went to Mexico and stayed a year. Later they returned to Texas, and have lived there ever since, mostly in Fort Worth. Griffin has continued his writing and public speaking, and his investigations of racism. His most recent book is *The Church and the Black Man*. Other works—fiction, non-fiction, an autobiographical account of his years of blindness—are in various stages of development. And his preoccupation now is with a biography of Thomas Merton, the noted Trappist monk and writer who died in 1968.

The Griffins live on a quiet suburban street in Fort Worth, in a rented house that looks to be of postwar vintage. Inside, away from the blowtorch summer heat, the sounds of

children and television and softly humming air conditioners
provide a background for the Mozart concerto coming from
the stereo, and the aroma of homemade bread baking—
Griffin is also a breadmaker of the first order—drifts from
the kitchen. In the back of the house is a darkroom, and
next to it a small office crammed with a desk and a couple
of chairs, filing cabinets and bookshelves, records and recording equipment and photographic paraphernalia. The walls
of the room are covered with his photography, which he
took up again after his blindness and still pursues with
avidity and great skill. The subject is people, the faces of
life: children and the elderly, peasants and paupers and
politicians, still life and vibrant life, prayer and protest.
Among the faces are Merton's and Maritain's, and there is
John F. Kennedy, and Saul Alinsky, and the Dalai Lama.
The photography is the most visible of Griffin's numerous
absorptions.

The man himself is relaxed, unpretentious, and a bit shy.
He is big—about six-feet-two and 200 pounds—with brown
hair graying at the temples and a soft, round face punc-
tuated by tinted lenses over gentle blue eyes. In the two
visits I made to his home, we talked mostly about race in
American society. This is part of what came from those conversations:

In being black, Griffin got more than an inside look at
the devastation of the black psyche in the South. For in
addition to experiencing the destructive effects of racism on
Negroes, he also saw its crippling consequences among
whites, and both the viciousness of the premeditated cruelty
and the pervasiveness of unconscious dehumanization were
far greater than he had feared:

> Negroes have suffered from discrimination imposed upon
> them by whites, and they have also suffered from a self-im-
> posed discrimination. Sensitive men whose humanity has been
> repeatedly denied have often developed feelings of contempt
> for their color, as if it were the cause of their misery. They

have blamed themselves, and many of them, before they have come to see who is really at fault for their plight, have been crushed and shattered. The white man would not let them be men. They couldn't protect their women, or hold good jobs, or give their children a model to live up to. They were unable to function as men in such profound ways that no man could stand himself. And in order to survive, they have had to submit to further degrading experiences—bowing and fawning and grinning, being court jesters, Tom-ing it, whatever was necessary to survive. It still goes on today, often in more sophisticated ways; aping whiteness, and denying blackness, is still a virtual requirement for most black men who want to "make it" in this country.

This, says Griffin, is what racism has done to countless thousands of black Southerners. The effect on whites, though altogether different, is just as destructive:

We live in a cultural prison of our own making. The open hatred, the vicious and depraved animal hatred of Negroes, has been repeatedy shown to the world by television and the press. It is not just ignorant people but educated ones as well who have been seized by this sickness. And yet, I do not minimize the massiveness of that evil when I say that the unconscious and unintended racism of a far greater number of white people is just as destructive. The distrust, the insults, the slurs, the countless acts and expressions perfumed with smiles—all of these say to the black man, "You are less than human," and they are more insidious and more insulting than a slap in the face. Undisguised hatred may be easier to deal with than ignorance. It's bitterly ironic that white people have said for so long that Negroes could not be equal because they are so ignorant, and now we find that it is the ignorance of whites which delays equality. We are so deeply immersed in the quagmire of white supremacy that we don't even recognize it, let alone know how to end it.

After *Black Like Me* was published, there were other revelations for Griffin. The repercussions in his home community were far greater than he had imagined they would be. "I thought there would be great resentment," he says, "but I was not prepared for the threats, or for the hatred directed at my parents." And equally as surprising, in a different way, was the mail he received. Of several thousand letters, only a few were derogatory. "Many of the letters were from the South," he recalls, "and they expressed tremendous anguish, and powerlessness, and fear of bucking the tide. As individuals, I believe we often feel the right thing, and we can even handle guilt, but as communities we are handcuffed by fear. We're afraid of our white neighbors. We're not free. And what costs doesn't get done."

Until his book came out, John Howard Griffin had a reputation as a sort of intellectual hermit who sometimes felt more at home in Europe than in America. His health, his temperament, and his scholarly interests dictated obscurity for him. He was surprised at the book's impact, and the notoriety he got from it was not altogether welcome. His solitary interests—music, writing, photography—had been accentuated by his blindness, and the fame which followed the book interrupted the solitude. Now, in spite of a heavy lecture schedule, he has regained some of the obscurity, and it suits him: "I belong to no organizations. I belong to no one, and I exclude no one. My vocation is for obscurity, for creativity in solitude. The hermit life appeals to me."

It is hardly a coincidence that the hermit life also appeals to Jacques Maritain, as it appealed to Thomas Merton; those two men have had more influence on Griffin's life than any others. They were influential in his conversion to Catholicism, and in his commitment against racism. Now he is writing Merton's biography. Of him he says: "Merton was an authentic mystic, a contemplative, and yet he was enormously advanced creatively. He was an extremely rough, earthy personality, a man of great contradictions. The virtue of consistency meant nothing to him. He never tried to convert anybody, to change anybody; he was completely open and accepting. People who never saw him considered him the best friend they had, and it wasn't spurious—he had a wealth of humanity, and he gave it freely. I'm sorry for everybody who didn't know him."

Griffin remains committed to his faith, but he is critical of the organized church. "Unmasked evil is not explainable in human terms," he says. "People are being driven away from the institutional church and deeper into their religion, their personal faith. The structure is too cumbersome, and too impersonal, and too uncommitted. It has failed so miserably to combat racism that people are turning away from it—and toward their faith."

The mood of black America has changed dramatically since *Black Like Me* was published, and Griffin believes the changes are more a source of hope than of despair:

> When Martin Luther King took his campaign to Chicago and led the open housing marches through Cicero, he destroyed the illusion that all the bad whites were in the South. Many blacks had blamed themselves for the failure of integration, and when they saw white racism in the North, they realized that segregation was a condition imposed by whites and integration was being presented to them as the only alternative. The integration whites had in mind was really a fragmented individualism, available to those blacks willing to separate themselves from the black man and enter the white world one by one. So blacks have come up with another alternative: self-determination. They are taking a huge disadvantage and with concepts of black power turning it into an advantage. They intend to end the domination of white people over their lives. Their rights have been taken by a massive act of fraud, and they intend to take them back.
>
> The white reaction to all this is very distressing. There is armed repression, and with it there have been efforts to drive Negroes to a strikeback. Black communities are surrounded by armed whites. And less repressive whites have abandoned the goal of equality because they are no longer wanted as leaders. The image of the white man leading the black man by the hand is no good anymore. Whites need to be dealing

with the racism in their own neighborhoods, but we seem un-
willing to do that. Racism is institutionalized in our society,
and violence against blacks is often institutionalized too, but
most whites show little concern for that—we're too busy worrying about black racism. We haven't taken white racism se-
riously yet.

Black and white radicalism among young people is not
separated in the public mind, or even in the press, but there
is a great difference. I'm very disappointed in the Students
for a Democratic Society. They're good analysts—they see the
flaws—but they're not healers. They stop thinking when the
walls start crumbling. They're fascinated by nihilism and
anarchy. It's all very abstract, very theoretical. They're trying
to use the black students, or ride on their coattails, but it
won't work. Most of the blacks in this movement are not out
to destroy; they want change, and they have specific goals.
Their demands on the universities are for more black students, a more realistic curriculum, and more institutional
commitment to social change. The advocacy and practice of
violence by white radicals bothers me terribly. They are
using violence as a tool, and as a toy. I oppose it, and I oppose it among blacks too—but I see far less of it there. There's
been no black attack. Whites have always armed defensively,
but when blacks do that, we call it violence. There are black
extremists who want revenge, racists who see all white men
as devils, but black rage and violence is a worry and a preoccupation among black people, and many of them wonder
how we can fail to be equally as concerned about the white
racism and white violence in our communities.

I'm a firm believer in black power, as I believe any man
who wants the good of the total community must be. I don't
want my children—or your children, or anybody's children—
to grow up to be racists. The separatist trend is a transitional
thing. The dream of real integration, of true equality, has
been blocked by whites. Black power is an alternative to race
war in the United States. Black people were offered a frag-
mented individualism which required them to deny their
origins, their roots, even deny other blacks. They saw that
whites would always dominate, that all the change would

have to be made by themselves and none by whites. They saw unconscious racism looming as something worse than the redneck variety, and they despaired, and some of them gave in to rage. But the mass of black people in this country are turning to militant self-determination, to pride in their blackness, which is not a color but a lived experience. They are turning to a solution which doesn't require them to confront whites as enemies and—most important—doesn't depend on the conversion of whites for their own salvation. They no longer need a concession of humanity from whites—they are asserting it. Once again, our humanity is being saved by black people. It isn't the first time in our history that black men have been the first to see clearly. It's distressing to see the gap between black thinking and white perception of it. So many black people are making the critical distinctions between militancy, power and violence, but so few whites are. Yet in spite of this lag in white perception, the new mood of blacks has actually reduced the potential for race war—and it may hold the cure for white racism.

It is a historic tragedy that nonviolence didn't work. The black man was trying to cure his white brother with it, but the white man wouldn't be cured. Nonviolent resistance has done more than we realize, though. I think history will show that it accomplished an enormous thing in men's souls. It didn't fail, it just didn't complete the job. Black power is a progression from it. It's the black's assertion of his humanity, and it requires us to confront one another as equals.

Langston Hughes put the prophetic truth in a few lines of poetry almost thirty years ago:

> Negroes,
> Sweet and docile,
> Meek, humble, and kind,
> Beware the day
> They change their minds!*

*From "Roland Hayes Beaten" by Langston Hughes, copyright 1948 by Alfred A. Knopf, Inc., originally published in *One Way Ticket* (1948) and reprinted in *Selected Poems* (1959).

Since the beginning of the civil-rights movement, the defenders of white supremacy have insisted that morality cannot be legislated, that laws can be changed but not minds, that the attitudes of the white race could and would withstand all pressure to change. Now, black Americans are shattering those illusions. *They* are changing *their* minds, as Langston Hughes said they would. The failure of whites to keep up with the changing mind of black America distresses John Howard Griffin, but the fact that black minds are changing gives him great hope. He is not a separatist, and he doubts that very many black people are either. What he believes in is equity. There are inevitable manifestations of self-segregation in the development of pride, confidence, and identity. They are positive manifestations, not based on any notions of inferiority or hatred or subjugation. Griffin sees the pattern clearly, and it gives him encouragement.

As white Americans are confronted with a new image of blackness, the capacity of the white mind to change becomes crucial. Griffin believes the South may have some hidden assets for the uncertain period ahead:

There is always the possibility that we are romanticizing the South when we talk about its assets. It may simply be ten years behind the North, a decade late in its development of sophisticated racism, and industrialization will take care of that lag. But if we are ten years or a generation behind, then we have an opportunity to avoid may of the North's mistakes. I don't know if we can come to that kind of wisdom. Racism is such an insidious thing—it seems that things have to become utterly critical before we see them, and then it's too late.

Nevertheless, there are elements in the Southern experience of both whites and blacks which could be assets for us. The South is home for black Americans. Many who have left it feel a great nostalgia, a regret, a longing for it, and among those who have never left there is a tremendous reservoir of *a priori* forgiveness, a kind of sadness. Vast numbers of blacks,

regardless of their education or their economic status, knew
whites were handicapped long before any whites realized it—
if we yet do. The blacks have had a great concern for the
white man with all his racial hang-ups. We haven't fooled
black people in the South, not ever. Behind their survival
masks, behind the grinning and the yessing, blacks have been
in agony over the ignorance of whites. The unmasked hatred
by blacks in the city ghettos is not yet duplicated in the
South.

As for whites, the unique cultural system of the South has
bred a tremendous ambivalence in those who come to question it. I am one of them. I feel a love for the South, and a
horror of it. But I will say this: the Southern white who does
come to grips with his racism comes to it more completely
than anyone else. It is overwhelming the way some Southerners are able to unload that dungheap completely. These
are the healers of the wounded soul and psyche of fellow
human beings, the ones who pray for the soul of the man who
killed Martin Luther King, instead of praying for King's soul.
Their number is small beside the tens of thousands of ruined
human beings, black and white, who would still be searing
our consciences even if justice came tomorrow, but they are
there, and they are the South's hope.

John Howard Griffin has been an expatriate from the
South more than once in his life. "I felt like a stranger in
the South for a long time," he says, "but not any more. I
identify more and more with the soul of the South." The
man who once was black is home to stay.

Billie and De De Pierce

Jazz, the experts say, is the only authentic art form to be born in America, and New Orleans was its cradle. So they say. I wouldn't know about that, but I do know that New Orleans jazz—what there is left of it—is a finger-snapping, hand-clapping, toe-tapping, soul-grabbing kind of music that speaks to me. It was created by black Americans, out of a fusion of field songs, hymns and spirituals, simple rhythms and melodies, and music of African and Creole inspiration. Their creation—which also included vocal and instrumental blues, a vital component of jazz—has spawned many other musical styles, including ragtime, swing, boogie woogie, bop, modern blues, progressive jazz, rock, and some gospel and country music; and many of America's greatest musicians owe their fame to the bass and brass and banjo and clarinet and piano sounds that have emanated from the French Quarter since before the turn of the century.

The French Quarter is still New Orleans' top attraction, even though commercialism has hidden much of its authenticity behind a façade of gaudy clip joints and bump-and-grind nightspots that cater to well-fixed conventiongoers and tourists, and most of the music that now echoes along Bourbon Street is a crude facsimile of traditional New Orleans jazz.

But you can find the genuine article a few steps off Bourbon, at 726 St. Peter Street. For a buck, you can squeeze into Preservation Hall with the rest of the aficionados from Dubuque and Toledo and East Orange and listen for three or four hours to some great old heads blowing a gig that can't be beat.

On a spring-like Monday night in early December, the little room was jammed. I found enough space to sit on the floor in front of the first row of chairs, almost under Louis Nelson's trombone, and I was rewarded with a kind of spiritual uplifting that included *12th Street Rag, Muskrat Ramble,* and *Just a Closer Walk With Thee.*

All of the musicians were black except the man on clarinet, and all of the audience was white except one couple sitting mesmerized on a bench against the side wall near the band. Between sets I asked them if they were from out of town. "No, man, we're from down here," the Negro man said. "We come to listen almost every night. This is my kind of music."

The people who call good jazz "my kind of music" are a richly varied lot, not separated by race or sex or economic status or social class or even age. One of the reasons the music is so contagious is that it draws its inspiration from so many sources. Its base is black and Southern, but there is French and Spanish and Creole in it, and it is shot through with religious inspiration and with the ageless themes of mirth and misery, love and joy, poverty and death. Its most famous artists have been men and women, black and white, from all sections of the country; it was five white guys in Chicago who put the tag "Dixieland" on it. Jazz is a universal and inclusive form of musical expression, a participatory thing for both the musicians and their audiences, a warm and highly personal kind of sound. Sure-enough jazz is sure-enough soul music.

But jazz is dying. It can be argued that the cause is a loss of talent, or the rise of other kinds of music, or a change in public tastes, but I believe these are only symptoms. In a way, you could say that jazz was doomed the minute it was born. It had a fatal disease: segregation. To be more precise, I should say that the music and the musicians were not segregated so much as the climate around them, and that climate has suffocated jazz and left it moribund.

Segregation and jazz came along at about the same time, near the end of the last century. The misery of Negroes under the yoke of white supremacy no doubt contributed to the creation of the music, and those who played it, particularly in later years and in cities outside the South, often were able to do so without suffering under the burden of racism. But it is an irony of tragic proportions that segregation stole jazz from the people who created it, distorted its impact on the masses to whom it was directed, and kept it from becoming the dominant and representative music of America. The Negroes from the South who have become most famous as jazz musicians—Louis Armstrong is the prime example— had to leave the South to make their mark, and even that did not exempt them from discrimination. For decades, the audiences to which jazz was played were either all white or all black, and it was in the white world that the music gained notoriety. All too often, the music was adulterated by buffoonery, shuffling, and slapstick, to conform to the white stereotype of "happy niggers." The management and promotion of jazz were in the hands of whites—still are—and they gained by far the most wealth from it. And the hundreds of great musicians who stayed in the South—many of them fully as talented as those who made the big time elsewhere—got little credit or compensation for what they did. Jazz became a commercial success for whites, and many outstanding musicians, including white non-Southerners, made it an artistic success as well. But the Negro Southerners who created it— in particular those who remained around New Orleans— could only watch with frustration and dismay while their soul music which could have been for all souls was split by segregation, leaving them and their devotees with an existence that made their blues authentic. They had their great Carnival marches and funeral dirges and street parades, but the fame and the real bread were in the company—and in the possession—of whites.

The vestiges of all that are visible now in what is left of New Orleans jazz. The most widely known musicians are Al Hirt and Pete Fountain, both white. The artists who play at Preservation Hall, all of them unexcelled jazz musicians, are mostly well past fifty, and if they are no longer dirt-poor, they still own no recording companies, no business enterprises, and no television contracts. Preservation Hall itself is owned and operated by white people, and when the bands go on the road they are booked and managed by white entrepreneurs. The audiences, too, are still almost all white. Genuine, traditional jazz and blues are seldom heard except where the old masters from New Orleans are playing, and their ranks have diminished to fewer than one hundred. The music is as great as ever, but it never became the major musical language of this country, because segregation got in the way.

Billie and De De Pierce were not playing in the seven-piece band at Preservation Hall the night I was there. They had just returned to New Orleans from a punishing, ten-week tour through the western half of the United States with their Preservation Hall Jazz Band, and they were at home resting from the rigors of that experience. Mike Stark had taken me to their house to meet them earlier that day, and we had ended up staying for several hours. Mike Stark is not a musician—he's a man with another bag—but he and the Pierces are close friends, and how that came about is a story in itself.

Stark is a thirty-year-old Texan who passed through New Orleans in 1962, on his way home from Louisville, where he had been to see about enrolling in the Baptist seminary there. Preservation Hall had been opened only a short time, and he wandered in there one night and fell in love with the music. "I had heard Dixieland before," he says, "but that has very little to do with this music." There is also a Baptist seminary in New Orleans, so he enrolled there, and by the time he left in 1964 he had spent so much time at the Hall that the Pierces, in Mike's words, "adopted me." He went back to Texas and worked for a few years in a mental hospital, and in 1968 he came back to the French Quarter and opened a gift shop—"Stark Realites"—on Bourbon Street, in partnership with two local businessmen. In addition to the shop, he managed an apartment building for a while and now has a health clinic, and in all three enterprises his clientele are mostly young "long-hairs" and hippies, "Easy Rider" kids, casualties of the Affluent Society.

In appearance, at least, Stark bears no resemblance to the pious country boy he once was. His red hair is thin on top but shoulder-length behind, and with his bushy red beard, a pair of sandals, and an ankle-length robe, he appears not unlike a balding, slightly overweight Jesus might look. Sometimes the garb is a red headband, a pair of bib overalls, and a red, white, and blue stickpin shaped like an American flag. It's a bit far out even for the Quarter, but Stark is actually a pretty straight sort of fellow. He doesn't drink, smoke, or cuss, doesn't use drugs or abuse women or play the horses. He is a combination counselor-chaplain-confessor to the youth colony in the Quarter, a sort of practical and spiritual feeder of the flock. That is part of his world. The other part is jazz, and the musicians who play it, and there the roles are reversed: it is the musicians who feed *him* spiritually.

Billie and De De sometimes provide him with other forms of nourishment too, like red beans and rice, or spicy hot cabbage, or filé gumbo. The day we went it was cabbage and rice and pigtails, and Mike put away a generous portion while we sat around the kitchen table in their tiny house on Galvez Street. The house sits behind a large residence which they own but choose not to live in. De De and his father built the family home many years ago, and it is occupied now by several of his relatives, all of whom were in and out of the Pierce kitchen while we were there. It was an afternoon and evening of lively, animated discussion, spiced with "integrated" Scotch (Black and White brand) and cabbage and rice and strawberry soda pop and apple pies from the neighborhood bakery and jazz on the phonograph and an impromptu performance of piano playing and singing by Billie. It was a happening, and it was a rare experience.

De De Pierce has been blind for fifteen years now, a victim of glaucoma. He is sixty-six years old, a native of New Orleans, and a trumpet player extraordinary. His father was a brickmason and his mother was a seamstress, and they were Creoles, part French, part Spanish, part Negro. De De (his real name is Joseph LaCroix) learned from his father to lay bricks and taught himself to play the trumpet. After he finished eighth grade he quit school and spent all his time on music and masonry. "My father was one of the best and fastest bricklayers in the state of Louisiana," he said. "He was head builder for the city of New Orleans—he built the old courthouse down on Chartres Street. He was gifted at his trade, a gifted Negro, a brilliant man. And he was respected, because he was able to produce. I trained under him, and we worked together for many years, me layin' brick by day and playin' in the Quarter at night. My mother was schooled in a convent. She spoke fluent French and Spanish, and very little English. So I grew up knowin' how to speak English and French and Creole and jargon." Those influences are evident in much of the music he has composed and arranged and sung, including *Eh La Bas,* a jazz classic.

Billie was born in Marianna, Florida, and grew up in Pensacola. Her father was a railroad man, and he and her mother both played the piano, and so, in time, did Billie and her six sisters. "Music's been my life," she said. "We were Baptists, and I played a lot of hymns and spirituals, as well as blues. Bessie Smith, the great blues singer, brought a show to Pensacola when I was about fifteen, and when her piano player got sick she came lookin' for one of my sisters. I played the *Gulf Coast Blues* for her, and she said, 'Honey, I like the way you play.' So I played her show for a week, and from then on that's all I wanted to do."

She made it to New Orleans in 1929, when she was twenty-two years old, and six years later she met De De, who was playing in a band with one of her sisters: "I fell for him, that ain't no lie. I told him, 'De De, I love the hell out of you, baby,' and it wasn't long 'til we got married. And we went to work that same night, in our weddin' clothes. Those days we was workin' for six bits or a dollar a night. I don't regret none of them days—had less money and more fun than we've ever had."

Aside from a three-week tour of Negro theaters in Florida with Ida Cox and her band, Billie and De De stayed mostly in New Orleans. They played with a lot of bands and orchestras over the years, and except on rare occasions, the audiences were white. Looking back on those thirty-five years, they talk a lot about their good times together and about the satisfaction they have gotten from the music; of the grim realities of segregation and racial discrimination, they say very little. De De explained:

Life is better for Negroes today than it used to be, but in the neighborhood we lived in back then, we had white neighbors, and my mother and that lady used to pass food back and forth across the fence. Bein' a musician, I've been among the white and black, and I've made my livin' among the white, understand me. As far as bein' treated the same goes, it's been due us for a hundred years. That's the way I feel about it, as a Negro. I don't see why, if you dark and me white, I should treat you any different. There's good and bad people, black and white. It's all in your heart, it's how you feel.

Billie added,

> If I stick my arm and you stick your arm, it's the same red, ain't it baby? People from all over come here and sit down, and they're welcome. Norman Thomas sat right at this table and ate my gumbo, and I had my picture made with him, me in an old print dress. This segregation is damn fool business, it's nothin' but ignorant bastards doin' that. In New Orleans, you can't hardly tell who's who anyway, people have mixed so, and that's the way it oughta be, instead of puttin' on all them labels. Me, I get along, and I ain't had no trouble with anybody. I've always had a job, a friend, I could always make a dollar. Life's what you make it. I'm happy go lucky.

It is no doubt true that the Negro jazz musicians have had it better than the average black man on the street in New Orleans, or elsewhere. They've had the satisfaction of professional accomplishment, a certain amount of fame, and a fairly steady financial return, and not many Negroes were that fortunate in the quarter-century between the Depression and the start of the civil-rights movement. In the days of the Movement, jazz and the black musicians who played it were often criticized as Uncle Toms by many black and white liberals. In retrospect, the label seems thoughtlessly cruel; the black community in New Orleans has had—and still has—a strong and identifiable culture of its own, an indigenous black pride, and one of the dominant reasons for that is the tradition of music. Says Mike Stark: "Street parades and funeral marches are major events here, and I think that partly explains why we haven't had violence. Back when denying blackness was in vogue, New Orleans blacks were out in the street celebrating life; some people said they were clowns, shufflers doing minstrel stuff; but the black community here doesn't agree, and they're right. There has been a lot of creative accomplishment here, and the tradition around that is a great source of pride."

Still, segregation and discrimination persisted. There were occasional exceptions for some of the black musicians, and there was the joyful abandon of Mardi Gras, but for most Negroes the reality of white supremacy was constant. What is more, while jazz could be claimed as theirs by black New Orleanians, their brothers elsewhere could see it as just another example of white thievery.

In 1961, the number of traditional jazz and blues artists in New Orleans was down to less than 150, and many of them were finding it hard to get steady work at union scale. Larry Bornstein, who came to New Orleans from Wisconsin thirty years ago and now owns a lot of French Quarter property, had a place called "The Patio," where a number of the musicians congregated. Bornstein and a young tuba player from Philadelphia named Allan Jaffe were the principal figures in a jazz-preservation movement that evolved into Preservation Hall, which Jaffe and his wife now operate. Between it and Dixieland Hall—a similar enterprise in the Quarter which leans more to commercialism and the confirmation of stereotypes—most of the old pros of the jazz world are provided with steady jobs at union wages, and a chance to make a bigger haul from records and road shows.

But the number of musicians still able to play is less than half what it was nine years ago, and no young stars are coming along. The Japanese, who have a penchant for imitation —often with results that are an improvement on the original—are now trying their hand in the jazz field, but they are not likely to make a major success of it, at least not in this country. And for all the credit Bornstein and Jaffe deserve for their salvation of jazz, the pattern remains as it always has been—black musicians playing for white audiences, to the primary financial benefit of white promoters.

The Pierces see that; all of the musicians do. They have

seen it since they first began to play. They have seen people like Louis Armstrong leave the South and still find themselves playing in clubs and hotels where they were not allowed to eat or sleep. They have seen Elvis Presley become a living legend and a multimillionaire, while Little Richard, who did it first and maybe better, is now a forgotten man. They see Al Hirt and Pete Fountain rising to fame and wealth. It is nothing new.

But the pot is sweeter now. Since the opening of Preservation Hall, many of the musicians have made world tours, they've cut records and played concerts all over this country, and they are in better financial condition than they've ever been. Sometimes they are asked why they don't have their own recording studios, or why they don't do their own booking (they get 25 per cent of the take from a road trip), and the answer De De gives to that is probably typical. "All I wanta do is blow my gig," he says. What keeps them going? Well, they love the music, they're hooked on it. And, like all human animals, they like applause and approval, the feeling of being appreciated and wanted. They feel an obligation, too, to reward that appreciation with good music, to reciprocate. Finally, they are kept going by the desire for material gain—and by their booking agent or manager or promoter, whose gain (and perhaps whose desire as well) is greater.

So they play in almost every state west of the Mississippi in ten weeks' time—concerts, over fifty of them, mostly on college campuses, mostly one-night stands. For many of the kids, the music is something brand new—they've never heard it before—and they eat it up. Grand Forks, Billings, Cheyenne, Seattle, Anchorage, Colorado Springs, El Paso— they all run together, the days, the towns, the crowds, the miles by bus.

"I've experienced the world, all over," says Billie Pierce. "Wherever we go is home for De De and me." They do not think of themselves as Southerners, yet they never considered moving away from New Orleans. Their way of life is built around that city, around the French Quarter and the music. They are simple, innocent, wise people, proud of who they are and what they can do. The complexities of politics and racism and human avarice are beyond their control, and they don't waste much time agonizing over them. But the music is something else—it is their idiom, their medium, and its message speaks for itself. "You can *feel* it, baby, anybody can feel it," Billie says. "I don't understand modern jazz. When *I* play, you can *understand* my music. Even in another language they can still dig me."

She went to the piano in their bedroom, next to the kitchen, and played and sang a dozen pieces, from hymns to boogie woogie. De De turned a vacant stare in the direction of the piano and smiled. "That's the *Outhouse Blues* she's doin' now," he said, "with a half-moon on the door." Nira Bowman, De De's niece, was there, and her husband Leonard, and their five children bounded in and out from time to time. Billie played *What A Friend We Have in Jesus,* and Leonard began looking around. "Where's that collection box?" he said.

Later, Nira put on a record of Billie and De De and their Preservation Hall Jazz Band. One of the songs was *Freight Train Blues,* with Billie singing:

I have a mind to stay here,
And a mind to leave this town.

How many million people have ever had that feeling? A mind to stay here, and a mind to leave this town, this land, this world. "This is one of the biggest joke cities there is," Leonard said. "What the hell is a Creole, what's white, or black, or colored? Billie there, she's part Seminole. De De, he's a Creole. What are you, De De?"

De De shrugged. "I'm a Negro," he said. "But what is that?" Leonard asked. Billie cut in. "In New Orleans, you can't hardly tell who's who," she said. "There's Creoles with dark skin, and there's Creoles with blue eyes and blonde hair. And there's the *passe blanc,* the guy who passes for white. They're the biggest trouble in this town. They don't want to mix with me and Nira and the rest of us. They won't associate with dark-skinned Negroes. The hell with them. I just let 'em know I'm a regular woman, I ain't tryin' to pass for *nothin'*."

"It's a crazy mixed-up world," Leonard said. "Ole Earl Long, when he was governor, he got to where he would talk about how mixed up we are, and they put him in the crazy house. He was gettin' too close to home for a lot of these cats. Like Leander Perez, who was the world's greatest hypocrite. Nobody's pure anything. But you still got a lot of people showin' their kids the color line, and you still got a lot of people sufferin' because of that."

The color line. People saying they are better than other people, drawing lines, building walls, separating according to skin color. It'll never work—but tell that to the black man who walks the streets of New Orleans, looking for work, or for a drink, or for revenge. Tell it to the man who can go for months from his suburban home to his air-conditioned bank to his country club and not speak to or hear a black man. Tell it to the more than one million black people of Louisiana, where there is a grand total of sixty-four black elected officeholders.

It is, indeed, a crazy mixed-up world. It is all too confusing, too impossible. Billie and De De Pierce have a framed picture of John and Robert Kennedy and Martin Luther King hanging over the piano in their bedroom. Some people would say that is as close as they have come to militancy, to protest, and they themselves would probably agree. They haven't marched in demonstrations, or made speeches, or gone to jail. They haven't identified themselves with the South, or with black power, or with the surge for human equality. In many respects, they are quite different from all the other people I have written about in this book. Yet they are proud, and they have produced something of value, and who is to say that anything else they might have done would have been more effective? Who can say that what *he* has done amounts to more?

In a very fundamental way, Billie and De De are fully Southern. It is where their roots are. They have seen the world from the windows of a bus, from a thousand spotlit stages, but New Orleans is home, and they come back to what is familiar, back to nurse their hurts and replenish their souls. When Billie says, "The South is like anywhere else, it's no different to me," maybe she is telling it straight, telling a truth that neither those who condemn the South nor those who defend it can bring themselves to face: the South *is* no different, no worse, no better. There is no Promised Land, no greener grass, no way out. There is nothing we can do to bring the millennium. It is out of our hands.

So what does that leave? For Billie and De De and all the other black masters and slaves of jazz, they can only play and sing their hearts out, only be who they are and what they are, and be that honestly, until the last trumpet sounds.

The South:
The Same, Only Different

One of the surest indicators of the rightness of the civil-rights movement ten years ago was its irrepressible sense of humor. In the young students who sat in at lunch counters and restaurants and theaters across the South there was such an unquenchable confidence and an intuitive sense of irony that humor became one of the movement's most effective weapons. Like the perfect squelch said to have been delivered to a waitress who told a sit-inner, "We don't serve niggers in here." The student's polite reply: "That's okay, I don't eat 'em. Just bring me some fried chicken, please."

And then there is the story of the Negro minister who left Mississippi for Detroit, where he became pastor of a large and very successful congregation. One night the Lord spoke to him, saying, "Mose, I want you to go back to Mississippi and lead my people. I need you there." The preacher was dismayed. "Lord, I don't know if I can," he said. "It would sure be hard. But if you need me, well. . . ." His voice trailed off, and then in a minute he said, "Please don't make me answer you right now, Lord. Just let me think about it a little." A couple of nights later, the Lord spoke to him again: "Well, Mose, have you made up your mind?" There was silence, then a sigh, and Mose said, "Yes, Lord, I'll go. But there's just one thing, one condition." The Lord asked, "What is that?" and Mose answered, "I'll go, if you'll go with me." There was no answer. Then, after what seemed a very long time, the Lord spoke. "Tell you what, Mose," he said. "I'll go as far as Memphis."

It was a great joke—until April 1968. Martin Luther King, in Memphis to march with striking garbage workers, was standing on the second-floor balcony of the Lorraine Motel when he was shot and killed by a sniper in a nearby building. "God must have chickened out on that trip," a man said, and then another asked, "But why does it say on Dr. King's tombstone, 'Free at last, free at last, thank God Almighty I'm free at last'?" Another irony, but no more humor. Humor is a rare commodity now.

Memphis. Part big city, part country town. Part Tennessee, part Arkansas, part Mississippi. Southern, but Midwestern too, connected to the "outside world" by the river at its door. Draw a 350-mile line along Interstate 40 from Nashville through Memphis to Little Rock. From points on or near that narrow strip in the last six months of the 1960s came these snapshots of the post-Movement South:

The Reverend James Bevel was in Nashville in 1959 at the start of the sit-ins, in Mississippi in 1962 at the start of voter registration, in Birmingham in 1963 at the start of the big demonstrations there, in Selma in 1965 at the start of that campaign. And he was in Memphis in 1968, at the end of the trail for Martin Luther King—he was standing at the bottom of the stairs, just below the balcony, when the shot was fired.

Bevel was in Memphis again in the summer of 1969, holding a revival at the Tree Of Life Baptist Church, and I saw him then in his room at the Lorraine Motel. During the course of an afternoon's conversation he talked about much that has happened to him since his childhood days around Itta Bena, Miss., and two subjects of that conversation stand out in my mind. One was the Southern influence in the civil-rights movement. The other was James Earl Ray.

Bevel was one of the organizers of the Student Nonviolent Coordinating Committee, but he joined the Southern Christian Leadership Conference in 1962 with the intention of trying to bring the two organizations closer together. The effort was unsuccessful, and Bevel finally parted company altogether with SNCC and devoted all of his time to SCLC. In his view, much of the conflict which divided the ranks in SNCC was basically a conflict between Northern and Southern philosophies.

I've always felt very comfortable in the South, more so than in the North. I've never had the intense fear of Southern whites. I've been confident, and I guess that's because of the influence of my daddy. He was an easygoing man, he never did get bitter, he never hit anybody, never had a gun —but he wouldn't let anybody walk over him.

The Northern boys in the Movement never got a feeling for the South—they didn't understand and respect the Southern dynamic. They thought that because black people in the South didn't spout off a lot of social philosophy they were stupid. Just because a man is out plowing with a mule doesn't mean he's a fool. It may mean he understands he's involved in a life process, and he enjoys it. Everybody who's not competing is not a fool—he may be wise.

Stealing is the norm in the North, but not in the South. Southern black people would give us food, and let us use their cars, their houses. The fellows from the North didn't understand that—they wanted to take advantage of it. They didn't see that the pattern among Southern blacks was basically communal, whether it was delivering babies or cutting stove wood for old ladies. When people said you could use their car, they meant for you to put gas back in it and return it on time. These smart cats from the North, they saw themselves as being real slick guys among a lot of dumb people, and they abused their right to be leaders. They tried to impose their Harvard-Howard education—white folks' education—on these people, and it never did work.

The Northern cats were trying to impose an abstract philosophy without understanding black people in the South. Take the black church, for example: "Thou shalt not steal," and "Love thy neighbor," and "We're all God's children," and "Clothes don't make you"—all that meant *being* black to us, instead of just *shouting* black. It was not a lot of superficial Western garbage about the social order.

The black kids in the South who got into the Movement weren't belligerent—they were just courageous, just quiet, simple, straightforward kids. They were courteous, but they weren't scared. Belligerence and bravery are not the same thing. The Northern cats would want to call the preacher a goddam Uncle Tom, or the sheriff a redneck sonofabitch, but the Southern kids would just say Mr. So-and-So, or Sheriff So-and-So. They had a calmness and a peace. Inner frustration was not a part of the life style of Southern black kids. The Northern kids were being aggressive out of frustration, not out of wisdom. They blew in here with that Northern accent, and they intimidated a lot of Southern cats, but it was just words, not knowledge. We were further ahead in our social thinking in many ways than they were. Like in black history, in black awareness—at least we had black teachers in our schools, and they were from our own communities, and they went to our churches. The whole question of North versus South was always a conflict in SNCC, right from the first.

Bevel himself has spent a good bit of time in the North —he lived in Cleveland for several years when he was a teenager, he was with Dr. King on SCLC's ill-fated open-housing campaign in Chicago, and more recently he directed a project for SCLC in Philadelphia. His view of the black South could hardly be called parochial. He didn't say that all the young people from the North who came into the civil-rights movement were "slick cats" with no understanding of the South, or that all Southerners in the Movement were honest and courageous and totally virtuous, and of course they weren't. But there *was* a fundamental difference in the way most Southerners and most of their Northern counterparts viewed the Movement and their role in it, and Bevel's interpretation of that difference is one that many Southerners—and even some Northerners—share.

The other thing I especially remember from our conversation was what he said about James Earl Ray. When Ray was in the Memphis jail awaiting trial for the murder of Dr. King, Bevel managed to get in to visit him. He also had some long discussions with Percy Foreman, who at that time was Ray's attorney. To the profound shock of many people, Bevel announced that he was convinced that Ray was not the killer. He said he thought he could prove that in court, and he offered to help defend Ray. Both Ray and Foreman seemed interested in the offer, but the state denied Bevel the privilege of taking part in the trial because he is not licensed to practice law.

In the motel that day, a few doors down from the spot where King was killed, Bevel reflected on the crime. "Ray didn't do it," he said. "He may have been involved, but not at a conscious level, not with foreknowledge. He didn't pull the trigger—he couldn't, he wasn't capable of it. Someone else did it—a pro. Ray was the fall guy. He was used."

He went on to say that James Earl Ray is slow of mind and foot, and that he would not have been either mentally or physically capable of conceiving the plot and carrying it out, at least not without a lot of help. But that wasn't the main point Bevel wanted to make. "There were a lot of people, including some church officials, who wanted vengeance for Dr. King's death," he said. "Some of them just wanted a lynching. And there were some state and federal officials who wanted to convict Ray quickly, pin the whole rap on him, and then close the books on the case. Nobody much talked about finding the truth, or showing mercy, or doing justice. Nobody much said that whoever killed Martin was his brother. Everybody just wanted the man convicted, as if that would take care of things."

Ray was convicted. He pleaded guilty, and hinted at a

conspiracy, and he was given a life sentence and spirited away in the middle of the night to a maximum security cell in the state penitentiary in Nashville. And that "takes care" of James Earl Ray—but it doesn't take care of the question of whether he killed King, or whether he *alone* committed the crime, and it doesn't mean justice has been done, and it hasn't put an end to killing. All it means is that King is dead, and Ray is in prison, and life goes on, and there is no explanation for what has happened, no answer, no solution —and no assurance that any of it will make any difference. If Martin King is "free at last," then what are we?

An outside consulting firm made a study for the Memphis Area Chamber of Commerce in 1969 and reported that the city had a bright future—if it would take care of some unfinished business. The most difficult problem in Memphis, the report said, "involves the status and aspirations of the black community. This is no longer simply a matter of 'race relations' (although effective relations between the races are indeed essential to any solution of problems). What is needed —and this is set forth here strictly within the context of economic development—is a coming to grips with the deficiencies that characterize the physical environment, the training and educational facilities, the economic opportunities, and the public participation of the black community."

Deficiencies in employment, education, and housing were spelled out in the report, which also said that "at the top level of white leadership . . . there still seems to be less than full appreciation of the critical seriousness of the deficiencies that have to be overcome."

After that report was issued, there was a strike of workers —most of them black—at one of the hospitals in the city, and it was the second hospital in Memphis to be struck that year. There was also a black boycott of the school system, which is about 50 per cent black but has an all-white governing board, and desegregation became an issue again in the courts. A strong and assertive group of leaders was emerging in the black community, and one among them was the Rev. James Lawson, who ten years earlier had organized workshops in nonviolence for students protesting segregation in Nashville—and who was expelled from the Vanderbilt Divinity School as a result. Now, Lawson and the Rev. Ezekiel Bell and Jesse Epps, a labor leader, and other black Memphians were telling their city it had to change, and even the Chamber of Commerce was being told as much by its own consultants, and Memphis *had* changed, was changing, but it was all very late, and very slow, and everything was so much more complex and subtle and sophisticated than it used to be.

There is a young black man in Memphis named Lance Watson. He goes by the nickname of "Sweet Willie Wine," and he is known around town as the leader of an outfit of young militants called the Invaders. In the summer of 1969 he went to Forrest City, Arkansas, at the invitation of a black protest leader there to join in demonstrations against racial discrimination in employment and in the administration of justice. Further west along Interstate 40, at the state capitol in Little Rock, Governor Winthrop Rockefeller approached the Forrest City dispute in a way that contrasted sharply with the actions of his predecessor, Orval Faubus. In 1957, Faubus called out the national guard to prevent the desegregation of a Little Rock high school, and that became the first major battleground of the civil-rights movement. When Rockefeller's turn came, he met with the black leaders, made a trip to Forrest City to hear all sides, and put the weight of his office behind a campaign at the state level to attack problems such as the black leaders in Forrest City had brought to the surface.

The leaders had been planning a "poor people's march" to the state capitol, but after Rockefeller intervened they put it off. "Sweet Willie Wine" then decided he would make his own "walk against fear," and on a hot August morning he set out from West Memphis, accompanied by a handful of followers, five cars of state policemen, and a dozen newsmen. They passed through Forrest City on the way to Little Rock without incident, but further along the line the mayor of the little town of Hazen called up a 125-man auxiliary police force and ordered the highway through the town barricaded with farm implements. The mayor later reconsidered and had the barricades removed before Watson and three middle-aged Negro women—one of them reading aloud from the twenty-third Psalm—walked slowly through the middle of the town. On the sidewalks, white teenagers flashed the "V" for victory sign to Willie, and then cheered when he returned it. The rest of the march was uneventful, and when it was over, Watson said of the state troopers who had accompanied him, "If police were like this all over the United States, we wouldn't have any police brutality."

A few nights later, back in Forrest City, Watson and some of his followers were beaten by a mob of angry whites who had gathered outside the city hall to protest against the mayor and the police chief for what they considered too much leniency in dealing with black demonstrators. A white woman, the mother of seven children, was jailed that night (she had given aid and comfort to Watson and his followers during their march), and her husband served divorce papers on her while she was in jail and went on the local radio station to repudiate her publicly.

There followed a continuation of racial tensions in Forrest City—the national guard was called in by Governor Rockefeller for a time, a white boycott of desegregated schools was tried, and both black and white communities split into warring factions. At the end of September, a crowd of about 1,500 people, white and black, gathered in the local football stadium to hear the president of the

chamber of commerce and three ministers—two white, one
black—appeal for racial understanding and peace in the
community.

All of this happened in Arkansas in 1969 without the
presence of any major civil-rights organizations, any indig-
nant preachers or college students from somewhere else, any
representatives of the national press (except for a couple of
reporters who passed through at some point during the un-
folding of the drama). Nobody pays much attention to such
small-town skirmishes any more. Attention has been drawn
away from them to other places and other issues, and the
racial issues themselves have changed, from undisguised
white supremacy enforced by law to more subtle forms of
discrimination that are harder to detect but just as damag-
ing to the victims. But the Forrest Cities of the South may
well be more numerous now than they were at the height of
the civil rights movement. Most of them are local, indigenous protests by black citizens still seeking nonviolently for
the rights guaranteed them by the Constitution. They are
an unseen side of the contemporary South.

East along Interstate 40 from Memphis, another Southern
town was in turmoil. Somerville, Tennessee, had been in the
headlines back in 1959 when a group of Negro tenant farmers, evicted from their white-owned homes for registering
to vote, set up a tent city to wait out their appeal for justice
in the courts. The Fayette County Civic and Welfare League
was formed to provide support for the displaced farmers, and
two of the principal figures in that organization were John
McFerren, a black merchant, and his wife, Viola.

Ten years later, racial wounds were opened anew when
two white men went to the home of a Negro farmer and
severely beat his sixty-two year-old wife and two of their
daughters. A Somerville grocer and his son were charged
with assault in the beating; the son pleaded guilty and was
convicted in juvenile court, where the judge placed him on

probation to his parents. His father was bound over to the grand jury.

The Original Fayette County Civil and Welfare League called a mass meeting which was attended by about 1,500 Negro citizens, and a boycott of the entire white community was voted.

More than two-thirds of Fayette County's citizens are black, yet most of the country's schools, government offices, official boards, law enforcement offices, public accommodations and churches are still segregated. Ten years of off-and-on protest by blacks has produced little change in the white-dominated community; the beating of the three ladies signaled the beginning of a new phase in the struggle.

The McFerrens, still prominent in the affairs of the civic league, turned to the Tennessee Council on Human Relations for help, and Baxton Bryant, the council's executive director, went to Somerville. From mid-August until November he spent most of his time there, and during that period Somerville was reminiscent of the civil-rights protests of an earlier day. There were protest marches every weekend by local blacks and people from outside the community who came primarily in response to Bryant's recruiting efforts. Among the outsiders were some familiar faces from the civil rights movement, including John Lewis, James Bevel, James Lawson and Dick Gregory, and "Sweet Willie Wine" Watson came too. There was harassment by local police officials, who used billy clubs and fire hoses to break up marches, and the number of arrests mounted beyond the 500 mark as the weeks passed. One young Negro was wounded by gunfire, others were threatened by armed white men, and on the night after one rally shots were fired into the McFerrens' store, missing Bryant by a few feet. The boycott was highly effective. Tennessee Governor Buford Ellington sent representatives to the area on several occasions, but in contrast to Arkansas's Rockefeller he remained personally aloof.

Especially in the early weeks of the Somerville protest, the
parallels with the old civil-rights movement were striking.
In essence, what was happening there involved local blacks
united with blacks and whites from outside the community
in a nonviolent, biracial assault on white supremacy. Baxton
Bryant is personally symbolic of the old style, and so are
John and Viola McFerren. Bryant is a white man, a Texan
who once came within an eyelash of winning a Congressional
seat from Dallas. He is a Methodist minister, and he is totally committed to the goal of full equity for all people. As
an organizer and an operator, he is skillful, fearless, and
more militant than a great many blacks. The McFerrens,
seasoned by a lifetime of struggle against white domination,
are not disposed to be put off in their demands for more
than just token change. They and Bryant appeared to have
the kind of working relationship that is rare, and it would
have been unusual even in the days when "black and white
together" was the theme of the movement. But in spite of
the unity of the protest movement, in spite of the success
of the boycott, in spite of the support of outside demonstrators and the absence of black separatism and the domi-
ance of nonviolence—in spite of all these things the white
minority would not yield its race-based advantage. As time
wore on, the weekend marches became smaller, and finally
ceased altogether. In December, the grand jury refused to
indict the white grocer who had beaten the three black
women, and he went free. A white deputy sheriff was shot
and killed by a black man, and another law officer then
killed the black man. Gray, gloomy winter was descending
on the flat cotton fields of Fayette County. Bryant and the
McFerrens stayed at the job of pressuring the white community, but despair and bitter resignation were evident among
many of the county's black citizens. Not a single white person in Fayette County had spoken out in favor of equality.
However much the protest may have involved both blacks
and whites, the fact remained that all of the white protesters

—including Baxton Bryant—were from outside the county; among the residents themselves, racial polarization was complete. White minority supremacy and black majority opposition—the immovable object and the irresistible force—stood face to face, as they had a decade earlier.

It is an open question which group, blacks or whites, is the more inescapably shackled by the legacy of segregation and white supremacy. At another point along that 350-mile stretch of Interstate 40, I have an old friend, a white man I have known for a good many years. We understand each other: he hates niggers, and I don't. He is a farmer, and a rather prosperous one, with more than 2,000 acres under cultivation. In a good year, he will turn a profit of around $40,000, but not every year is a good one—he is subject to the vagaries of the weather and the market, and the only certainties are the long hours and the hard work.

As recently as six years ago, there were twenty-seven black families living on his farm; now, there are fewer than half a dozen. Some of them left in search of the Promised Land, but most were displaced by mechanization—they were not needed any longer, so my friend let them go. The plantation style of life that has dominated the county in which he lives is breaking up, but the past is not easily disposed of. A majority of the county's residents are black, and in the schools the ratio of blacks is even higher. And the schools are being desegregated, under pressure from the federal government.

My friend and his pretty wife live constantly with the preoccupation of race. They are angry and afraid and uncertain of the future, uncertain even of the present—and they are trapped by the past. Both of them have lived there all their lives, and they cannot conceive of their community becoming a place where whites no longer dominate. Unconvincingly, they say that maybe the next generation will deal with the race issue better than theirs, but the next generation—including their own children—is getting little if any preparation for anything except white supremacy and hatred of Negroes.

When they speak of black people (saying "colored," or "niggers," or occasionally—and self-consciously—"nigros"), my friend and his wife speak in voices that are a mixture of bitterness and hatred and guilt: "We're just prejudiced, that's all there is to it. All the niggers we've ever known are so dumb, so stupid. You'll never make me believe they're as good as white people. They don't want to integrate, they're happy. They've been exploited, held back, and now it's too late. They could never catch up. I wish I could get out of here. If I ever do, I'll go where there's no niggers." I asked him why he didn't buy a spread in Montana, and his laugh was rueful and bitter. "Who'd help me farm it?" he said.

Their home is lovely, a cool, roomy, tastefully decorated place. On one wall of the family room, a copy of the Declaration of Independence is prominently displayed. "We hold these truths to be self-evident. . . ."

And finally, Nashville. In 1959, it was a fertile breeding ground for the civil-rights movement; in 1969, it was something else. Exactly what is difficult to say.

There were blacks in the state Senate and in the House of Representatives, and the Metro Council, the governing body for Nashville and Davidson County, had five black members out of forty (compared to eight out of every forty in the population as a whole). The state and local governments had human relations commissions, and there were one or two private organizations of the same sort. The local representative in Congress voted consistently for civil-rights legislation. In employment, in housing, in the public schools, in the once-white colleges and universities, in public accommodations, blacks could be seen in ascending numbers in areas where segregation barriers once had excluded them. Even in the Grand Ole Opry there were a few black faces, and there was one big-time star—a singer with the ironic name of Charlie Pride.

George Wallace carried the county with a plurality over Nixon and Humphrey. A fifteen-year-old school desegregation suit in federal court, dormant for most of those years, was opened anew with the charge that the much-touted Nashville Plan of desegregation had left most of the black schools all black and kept over 80 per cent of the white students in schools that were overwhelmingly white. A black superintendent in the United Methodist Church, expecting to move into a parsonage in an all-white suburb, discovered that the parsonage somehow had been sold to the white superintendent who formerly had occupied it, and it took a month of searching to find a home for the new official. Housing—and consequently, schools—in the affluent white areas of the city remained segregated. So did most of the more than 600 churches, and the major financial institutions, and the board rooms of the leading business enterprises. A group of students at Fisk, one of the four predominantly black colleges and universities in the city, seized a building to dramatize their demands for a totally black institution—meaning, apparently, a purge of all white faculty, administrators, trustees and donors, including foundations. A federal court was weighing the question whether an expansion of the University of Tennessee's night-school branch in Nashville would perpetuate segregation at another state university in the city—Tennessee State University—where virtually all of the students were black. The net effect on black citizens—and on a great many low-income whites—of such federal programs as urban renewal, model cities, the war on poverty, and the interstate highway system often seemed more negative than positive.

In the context of race, it is easy to say what Nashville was in 1959: it was segregated, locked up tight by white privilege. Ten years later it was a different city, in many ways a better city for both blacks and whites. But segregation and

racial discrimination and white supremacy were still there
—not raw and blatant and direct, as in the past, but dis-
pensed with deftness and finesse by realtors and personnel
managers and registrars, the gatekeepers of white affluence.
The clarity and simplicity of an earlier day's racial issues
had given way to haziness and complexity. As it entered a
new decade, Nashville was still bound by the curse of racism
—bound in different ways, perhaps, than Somerville or
Memphis or Forrest City or the rest of the South, but bound
all the same.

Along the road from Nashville to Little Rock lay the contemporary South in miniature. The king of nonviolence
was dead, killed by a violent deed, and one of the king's
knights offered to defend the accused killer. Some people
were saying that nonviolence itself was dead, but old hands
in the quest for justice were still trying to bring sight to the
blind and deliverance to the captives, and their weapons
were reason and persuasion and appeals to conscience—not
guns and fire, not yet. In remote and scattered places there
were rallies and demonstrations and mass meetings, as of
old, and here and there appeals to black separatism were
made, mostly by students and other young blacks in the
cities. The race-baiting governors were gone, replaced by
some who tried, without much success, to heal racial wounds,
and others whose strategy was to do as little as possible to
alter the status quo. There was a "walk against fear"—an
idea borrowed from James Meredith—and this time it had
elements as bizarre and improbable as a screenwriter's fantasy: black militants from a city ghetto, a barricaded country town, a little lady reading the twenty-third Psalm aloud,
white youngsters cheering black marchers, marchers praising the police, white vigilantes beating blacks and threatening white officials, a white woman in jail being publicly re-
pudiated by her husband for lending aid to black protesters.
Blacks were being elected to public office—something new

—but others still died violent deaths at the hands of whites. Hatred and guilt and fear and fantasy still marked much of the white South's perceptions of Negroes, but the emotions were less overt, more subtle, more difficult to detect. Black emotions, on the other hand, were growing blunter, more direct and specific, more caustic and critical. The big cities were changed, for both better and worse. They were being told it would be good for business to provide black citizens with full equality—and the cities seemed no more moved by the logic of that than they had been by earlier appeals to morality and the law. More and more, they were beginning to look like their sister cities outside the South. The public schools, sixteen years after *Brown vs. Board of Education,* finally were facing total desegregation—if only because of the persistence of the federal courts. And the white churches: they, too, were different, but in many ways and to many people it seemed too late to matter. They were still laggard, still uncommitted to the fundamental, bedrock issues produced by racial estrangement. "A day of grace is yet held out to us," wrote Harriet Beecher Stowe in the last paragraph of *Uncle Tom's Cabin.* "Both north and south have been guilty before God, and the *Christian church* has a heavy account to answer." After 118 years, the account is still unpaid.

The South has changed, and it remains the same. So many different people, for so many different reasons, have seen it as a special place, a unique land, and it has been. At the beginning of 1970 it was in a state of becoming something it has not been, and everywhere it presented images of contrast, of paradox and irony and contradiction. The infinite combinations of human chemistry which give people and places their distinctiveness can also obscure and diminish that distinctiveness, and that is happening to the South. Whatever it ceases to be, whatever it remains, whatever it becomes, it has qualities worth preserving—beauty and dignity, generosity and hospitality, informality and human concern, a sense of humor and a sense of community. It is comforting to cling to the hope that those qualities might survive urbanization and industrialization and depersonalization, and provide the key to justice and human equality for us all. It is a faint hope, though, and getting fainter.

DATE DUE

GAYLORD			PRINTED IN U.S.A.